HOW
TO LIVE
BEYOND
YOUR MEANS

TAPPING GOD'S RESOURCES

HOW TO LIVE BEYOND YOUR MEANS

by
RUSS JOHNSTON
with
MAUREEN RANK

Tyndale House
Publishers, Inc.
Wheaton, Illinois

The Cassette Packet,
"How to Live by Faith,"
based on the material
from this book, is available
for $10 prepaid from
World Outreach for Christ,
1104 Cenotaph Way,
Colorado Springs, CO 80904.

Scripture quotations in
this book are from
the Revised Standard
Version unless otherwise
indicated.

Library of Congress
Catalog Card Number
78-57966.
ISBN 0-8423-1524-1,
paper. Copyright © 1979
by Tyndale House
Publishers, Wheaton, IL.
All rights reserved.
Second printing, November 1979.
Printed in the United
States of America.

CONTENTS

*To my dad, Maurice, whose hard work
and generosity created an abundance
of opportunities for me and my
five brothers and sisters.*

ONE
INCREASE YOUR MEANS
BY FAITH

*But Jesus looked at them, and said to them, With men
this is impossible; but with God all things are possible*
(Matthew 19:26).

When a friend here in Colorado Springs told me that last
year he took in $2000 more than his paycheck, I took
notice because I knew he hadn't taken on a second job; his
wife hadn't gone to work; and they weren't in debt.
The extra income, he told me, had come from God's
provision as they had learned to trust him. They were
living beyond their means because they were living by
faith. That same experience is happening to others, too.

Bill and Kathy McKenzie started their new house in
August, and the projected completion date was supposed
to be around the third week in October. They waited
until October 5 to sell the house they were living in, and
packed up their two kids to move in with Bill's
parents for the last couple of weeks until the house was
completed.

It was a neatly thought out plan, but the house didn't
get done on time. Finally, by November 15, the inside of
the house was finished, but the monsoon season had

begun in Oregon and the house looked as if it was anchored in the middle of a mud pit. The driveway needed to be poured before they could move in, and it couldn't be done until the rains stopped. And the only day in weeks that the rain let up, no one showed up to work on the driveway.

Bill's parents' house had just two bedrooms, and the two kids were getting cranky after weeks of sleeping on the living room floor and having no place to play. Bill's folks were exhausted and Kathy was depressed.

But a couple of weeks later, Bill and Kathy decided to take the weather and the driveway problem to God, asking that the driveway would be completed *that week*.

"I had some real doubts about giving God a deadline," Kathy admitted, "but I felt he was leading me. And I was also impressed that I had to tell people that God was going to work. So I stood up in the Sunday evening service at church and told everyone that I believed God was going to get our driveway poured that week.

"My spirits were really high as I faced the week ahead. Monday it rained as usual, but this time as I passed our 'Mud Hole' I told God, 'I believe you.' Tuesday it rained again, but I just repeated my prayer of faith. God had really given me a new attitude to replace the depression I'd felt before I started trusting him.

"On Wednesday the skies were clear and a bulldozer operator began preparing the ground and laying the forms. But they didn't pour the cement that day and the weatherman forecasted rain for the next day, so I just repeated my 'I believe' prayer."

Thursday morning the skies were threatening, but the cement men had decided to start work early. They finished pouring the driveway about 9:30 A.M., and they said that if the cement had about four hours for the surface to harden, it'd be fine. Four hours later, at 1:30, it began to rain.

Living by faith can make a difference in your business, too. When Lyall started selling real estate in Winnepeg four years ago, business was going well, but about six months after he got married, he seemed to lose all ability to sell. Lyall stuck it out in real estate the next two years, though it was only by his wife's salary that they kept from going under financially. He told me that in those two years he earned $5,200 and $3,600—not exactly prosperity. He tried looking for other work, but God had promised to prosper him in real estate, and nothing else opened up.

Then Lyall and Claire heard about activating their faith in God. And Lyall had an idea of how they could show God they were expecting him to work for them. Another realtor he knew had had some advertising printed up, but he hadn't distributed it because it was cold and he was busy. So Lyall sat down with him and offered to hand out the advertising for him. As they talked, Lyall shared his relationship with Christ and the faith principle of trusting God for your business. Lyall recalled, "After he picked up his teeth, he said, 'Fine. Go ahead and advertise for me if you want to.' Anybody could see that that was an offer not to refuse.

"One week later I told him I had finished giving out his advertising on a particular street. And he smiled. 'Thanks. It seems to be working for you, doesn't it?' "

Obviously it *was* "working." Clients for Lyall started coming out of the woodwork. "Friday morning I spent fifteen minutes handing out the other realtor's advertising, and at noon on Monday a prospective buyer was referred to me. Tuesday I spent twenty-five minutes on the advertising, and Tuesday night I got a listing. Wednesday a client phoned to say he would probably be selling in the spring. Thursday a contact phoned to say he wanted to sell his house and buy a new home. Friday I spent about twenty minutes advertising, and that weekend I got a referral from a

friend. I contacted the fellow, and he's going to
sell and buy. A friend of mine down the street from him is
also going to sell and move closer to the city, making
another listing for me.

"A deal I was working on ran into a snag, and I thought
it was lost, so I went out and gave out some more
of the other salesman's advertising. My client phoned
that night and clinched the deal."

One step of faith can lead to a lot of others. Lyall told
me, "We've sent in applications for a Christian
couples conference in Colorado for next summer, but in
order to go we have to pay off our debt ($1,800),
buy a new car (cash only), and have about $1,000 vacation
money. That's all over and above what I made last
year—and I must make it this year before June. We are
planning our trip and are quite confident that we'll
be going."

And I'm sure they will.

God doesn't honor faith only by giving you the
"essentials" like food and clothes. Looking to him as your
supplier can result in "extras," too.

If you don't agree, ask Bev Wannanger.

After a faith seminar Bev decided to list the things she
wanted to be currently trusting God to supply. Most
of the things she wrote down were necessities,
but at the end she added a silver tea set, just because
she'd always wanted one. She'd often wandered
through the silver departments of stores and wished, but
silver sets aren't exactly *need* items—and they are
expensive.

A month later, Bev heard that Betty Crocker was
closing out the stainless silverware pattern that her
church had been collecting for the church kitchen,
so she decided she'd give some stashed-away money to
the silverware project—as a reminder to God that
she was trusting only him to give her the silver tea set
she'd asked for.

A few days later, when a big department store nearby
sent out an ad about their silver tea sets being
on sale, Bev's husband decided he'd like to get her a set to
celebrate their upcoming fifteenth wedding anniversary.
Bev was delighted, but still a little reluctant because
of the amount of money involved. When they got to
the department store to pick out the set, a saleslady
pulled them aside. "I don't know if you noticed,"
she said, "that one of these sets was priced incorrectly in
the ad—but we're selling it for the ad price anyway.
The sale price is actually supposed to be $100 more than
the ad says." So Paul and Bev went home with a silver
tea set at $150 less than the regular price.

Lots of stories. Lots of ordinary people. But what they
have in common is that they all started with a need,
looked to God to provide, and activated their faith. In
each instance, God took care of the essentials; he
lifted the burdens; he even gave them some *un-needed*
wants!

And these believers are just a few of many. For
example, a businessman I know was hoping to sell his
company for $100,000, but he got six times that
price for it—by faith. And a homemaker told me how she
had wanted to start a Bible study with her neighbors, so
she prayed that women would *ask her* to lead a study
instead of her inviting them. Eight did and five
accepted Christ.

A couple I met in South Africa were trying to sell an
impossible house. It had been handled unsuccessfully by
six realtors already and was in the wrong location.
And with South Africa's discriminatory racial policies,
the wrong location means the *wrong* location. But
soon after they had learned in a faith seminar how to
activate their faith in God, I got a telegram: *"SOLD THE
HOUSE!* Love, Allister and Elizabeth." Elizabeth
wrote me later, "It's so easy to talk to people about God
now. All we do is tell them how good he is."

Each of these learned to quit living within their means —and start living within *God's* means by aggressive, activated faith.

And it can happen for you. You can find your needs met and your desires fulfilled as you learn to activate faith in God as your total resource. Quit living within your means and start living by faith!

TWO
JESUS, THE AUTHOR
AND FINISHER OF YOUR FAITH

Looking unto Jesus the author and finisher of our faith
(Hebrews 12:2, KJV).

The radio announcer had just finished interviewing me
for his talk show, so after the taping I figured it
should be my turn to interview him, and I asked him if
he'd thought about his relationship to Christ.

"Sure, I've thought about it," he responded willingly,
"but I'll tell you one of my hang-ups. A guy I know
got religion—you'd say he became a Christian—and gave
up a good job here in town to work for a Christian
radio station. They're so understaffed over there that he
can't get a vacation. He needs to trade cars, and
he'd like to get married, but his salary is so low that he
can't afford either one. If I commit myself to Jesus,
is that the kind of lifestyle I'm going to have to settle for?"

Inwardly I groaned. A well-meaning Christian with
a too-small picture of God had given this man a wrong
concept of the Lord.

Your God-picture matters. It determines your desires,
your direction, your personality, your relationships,
your lifestyle. In the book *Knowledge of the Holy*,

A. W. Tozer wrote, "What comes to our minds when
we think about God is the most important thing about us.
We tend by a secret law of the soul to move toward
our mental image of God. Were we able to extract from
any man a complete answer to the question, 'What
comes to your mind when you think about God?' we might
predict with certainty the spiritual future of that man."

HOW DO YOU SEE GOD?

Because their daughter was having reading problems,
a California couple took her to a well-known reading
specialist to try to determine the cause. The specialist
administered a variety of tests, but one of the
simplest and most revealing was "Draw the Man." What
Janet drew told much about her because her picture
showed a very, very small man in the middle of the large
sheet of blank paper.

With that drawing, the specialist reported, Janet
revealed much of her problem: she saw herself as a small,
insignificant person in the middle of a very big
world. Because she felt inferior, she was afraid of doing
any wrong thing—afraid she'd expose her inferiority. So
when she saw a big word in a sentence, she assumed
she probably would not be able to pronounce it—and
she froze.

I wish we could give a "Draw the Man" test to everyone
in the world. The only change would be that instead
of drawing a man, you'd have to draw your picture of God.
If I gave you a piece of paper now and told you that
was your assignment, what would you come up with?
Would you draw a General Patton with cleaner language?
A Charlton Heston-like Moses smashing the Ten
Commandments in anger against people's sins or a
wealthy Howard Hughes, wheeling and dealing and
manipulating people at the whim of his passing, selfish
fancy? Would you draw God as a face on Mount

Rushmore—inspiring to look at, but not much good in everyday life, or would the picture be the E-Z Credit Corporation—good for a quick loan in a pinch, but ready to repossess your house is you don't keep up your payments?

Recognizing your God-concept isn't all that difficult. The Psalmist explains how it's done: "The heathen worship idols of gold and silver, made by men—idols with speechless mouths and sightless eyes and ears that cannot hear; they cannot even breathe. *Those who make them become like them!* And so do all who trust in them!" (Psalm 135:15-18, TLB) If you want to know how you really see God, just look at your lifestyle. How you live and make decisions shows what you think God is like. With gods that couldn't see, hear, or breathe, the heathen of Psalm 135 were powerless because their gods were powerless. Thus they were easily frightened and intimidated.

Are you critical of others? You probably think God is critical of you—that he's a perfectionist who can't be comfortable with you or anyone else until your life looks like "The Impossible Dream." Is it hard for you to be generous? You probably see God as stingy with you, so you have to be careful what you give in order to keep enough to meet all your needs. Are you overworked? Your god probably doesn't care enough about you to dig in with you at your job or in your housework, or else he places demands on you that are beyond your capacity. If you have trouble praying, you probably don't believe God can or will act in response to your prayers, the way he promised he would.

ACQUAINT YOURSELF WITH GOD
The solution is an easy one—and a lifelong venture. "*Acquaint now thyself with him* and be at peace: thereby good shall come to thee' (Job 22:21, KJV).

Knowing God for who he really is—that changes people.

A lady I met in Swaziland, Southern Africa, told me that thirteen years ago she gave her life over to Satan. As she thought back over the twelve years that followed, she could not remember having two encouraging days in a row.

"But then I discovered Jesus Christ as he really is," she beamed, "and he keeps me on a high more consistently than anything else I ever tried."

Incidently, this woman was not a native from some primitive jungle tribe. She was a Peace Corps worker from Boulder, Colorado.

Not long after meeting her, I visited a private diamond prospector near Kimberly, South Africa, who had about thirty Africans working under him, mining for diamonds in the river sand. And he told me about taking over the operation two years before.

"This work camp was a bloodbath when I came. There was so much fighting and knifing going on that when one ambulance would be going to town carrying an injured man, it would meet another ambulance coming out to the camp to pick up someone else who'd been hurt. I had to do something.

"So I contacted a gospel preacher from one of the tribes, and asked if he would come out here every Sunday and tell the men about God. They started meeting over there under a tree every Sunday, about a hundred of them.

"I can't tell you how many of them have decided to turn their lives over to Christ," he concluded, "but somehow that exposure to God and who he is, is making a difference. We haven't needed an ambulance out here in a year now."

In the last faith seminar I taught, one man who attended was so negative that we talked about asking him not to come to the class anymore. His "down"

attitude was pulling everyone in the class down with him.
God intervened. One day in class he stood up, excited.
"I've been wanting outdoor camping equipment and
I started wondering what might happen if I put my desire
together with what we've been talking about of
God and his goodness. This week my brother-in-law came
by and gave me some camping equipment—worth $50!
I just had no idea God could be that good."

After that class, two different people mentioned to me
what a change they'd seen in this man's negative
attitude. A new concept of God and his goodness will
automatically produce life changes.

Do you wonder why it's so easy to get a wrong picture
of what God is like? For one thing, your whole culture is
working against you. You weren't born in a society
of saints. Your neighbors, the people at work, your school
teachers, TV shows, newspaper stories, some
religious spokesmen, and perhaps even your parents have
been teaching you lies about God since Day One. If
they knew him as he really is, they'd be serving and
enjoying and loving and devoting themselves totally to
him. But since they aren't, you can pretty safely
assume that you're not in an atmosphere conducive to a
right God picture.

Our culture is a lot like what Paul described in
Romans 1. "They exchanged the truth about God for a lie
and worshipped and served the creature rather
than the Creator who is blessed forever!" (Rom. 1:25).
That sounds like a young Canadian I met during the
1960s who was talking about being right with a holy God.
"It isn't all that hard," he said casually. "Just
bring God down to our level, and then we'll be equal."
Our society is mixed up about God.

And the devil is hanging right in there, reinforcing
every one of these nutty ideas about God. "Satan,
who is the god of this evil world," Paul explains, "has
made him blind, unable to see the glorious light of the

Gospel that is shining upon him, or to understand the amazing message we preach about the glory of Christ, who is God" (2 Corinthians 4:4, TLB).

WHERE TO START IN KNOWING GOD

So where do you start in knowing God as he really is, so that your lifestyle can reflect him accurately? The place to start is easy. Begin by looking at what he says about himself in the Bible, and then let life's experiences reinforce what the Word reveals to you.

Take Nahum 1:7: "The Lord is good, a stronghold in the day of trouble; he knows those who take refuge in him." Or Psalm 33:5: "The earth is *full* of the steadfast love of the Lord." Or Psalm 68:19 (KJV): "Blessed be the Lord, who daily loadeth us with benefits."

Once you let God show himself to you through the Word, life's experiences begin to affirm what you've read. Like the lady who told a friend about "the thirteen times over the last few months when the Lord stepped right in when things were going badly and gave great victory." Notice she did *not* say it was the thirteen times the last few months when things were bad, and God almost let them down.

The reason why you must evaluate your life's experiences in light of the Word is that you can easily get the wrong teaching from life. You've heard the age-old questions about how a loving God can let a Christian father of five little children die. It's too easy to look at circumstances and draw wrong conclusions about God— that he is not good, or that he is not out for your best.

We're busy asking why about *bad* things when we should be asking why about the innumerable *good* things that come our way.

The issue of life is not so much the amount of your faith as it is *who or what you place your faith in*. And faith in God as he really is—in his goodness, kindness, generosity, and caring—can give life the sense and direction you've hoped for. Start with Jesus as the author of your faith.

THREE
MAKE A LIST

So faith by itself, if it has no works, is dead (James 2:17).

It was not because I had any interest in the subject that
I signed up for the college course in concrete. I did
it in desperation. The problem was that as a college
senior, determined to graduate, I was two credit hours
short in the agricultural engineering department. So I
pulled out the catalog, dug up the first two-credit
course in which I thought I could pull a decent grade, and
signed up. Looking back now, I guess I was lucky to
have started at the front of the catalog rather than at the
end, or I might have wound up with two credit hours
in zebra mating habits.

But that course in concrete was not a total loss. I did
gain one useful piece of information: the difference
between cement and concrete. Go ahead and laugh, but do
you know the difference? Cement, you see, is the
ground-up stone that comes in the big paper sack, while
concrete is the finished product that you find as a
sidewalk or a highway.

That information is significant because it's a great
illustration of faith. Cement is pure, but in that pure state

it's worthless. Not until it's mixed with sand and gravel and water does cement become of value. And that same principle applies to faith and works. Faith by itself —in its "pure" state—is worthless. The Bible calls it dead. But mixed with an act, faith becomes alive, useful, aggressive, productive.

A lot of things I'm not, and one of them is *subtle*. But I think I've found someone even less subtle, and that's James, the writer of a hard-hitting New Testament epistle. Take a look at James 2:14-26 and note what he says about faith and action. Your mental list will look like this:

> Faith needs action (v. 14)
> Faith by itself is dead (v. 17)
> Faith is shown by its actions (v. 18)
> Faith without action is useless (v. 20)
> Faith is made complete by action (v. 22)
> Faith and action go together (vv. 24, 26)

I've heard of repetition to get a point across, but this is incredible. James wants us to know beyond the shadow of a doubt that *faith needs doing* to bring it to life.

James, however, was not original in propounding this concept. As he wrote, his mind probably went back to all the times when Jesus in his public ministry talked about faith and, in the same breath, always tied it to action. Jesus spoke of faith to move a mountain; faith to feed five thousand; faith to heal an epileptic; faith to raise a little girl from death.

Did you know that God has given everybody faith? Paul wrote: "God hath dealt to every man the measure of faith" (Romans 12:3, KJV). But your faith was never meant to be like a Boy Scout badge, to dress up your Sunday suit. God has given you faith to use. He intends for you to put it into action to accomplish the dreams and plans that he and you have for your life.

I've never been much for family trees. Somehow I just do not turn on to whose Uncle Robert married Bertha Wilson's sister-in-law. That's also why I usually skip over those lists of genealogies in 1 Chronicles, but in the midst of those genealogies there's an interlude worth noting. God stopped for a minute in his listing of families to make a comment about a fellow by the name of Jabez. That comment comes in 1 Chronicles 4:9, 10: "Jabez called on the God of Israel, saying, 'Oh, that thou wouldst bless me and enlarge my border, and that thy hand might be with me, and that thou wouldst keep me from harm so that it might not hurt me!' and God granted what he asked."

God singled Jabez out for recognition when he said, "Jabez was more honorable than his brothers" (v. 9). And what great acts did he do to deserve commendation? He simply made a list of his three biggest desires in life. He wanted the borders of his country enlarged; he wanted God's hand to be with him; and he wanted to be kept from harm. Jabez put down his desires and then asked God to do them.

If you had been God, how would you have reacted to Jabez's request? Would you have yelled at him for being selfish, since the fulfillment of each of these desires would certainly result in personal gain to Jabez? Or would you have torn up the list and informed him that you had no intention of being used by him as a Super Santa?

The Scripture says simply, "... And God granted what he asked" (v. 10).

God said yes to Jabez because what Jabez did was the action, the doing that makes faith alive and productive. He took specific stock of his current needs and desires and then asked God to fulfill them. He made a list.

It seems that the life-changingest part of our seminar on how to live by faith comes during the ten minutes

in which the people are asked to pull out a piece
of paper and write down what they'd like to be doing or
to have accomplished in the next three months if
resources were no problem.

Open your mind to that one. What would you have or
be doing three months from now if resources—the
money, the time, the change in people's attitudes,
whatever—were all available? Would you be out of debt,
or leading a neighbor to Christ, or starting your
own business, or just what?

One young couple came up with a list of five things:
1. Replace their old car with a reliable one
2. More time for the husband with their three-
    year-old son
3. Get a new sewing machine with advanced
    features
4. Be totally positive about next year's job
    assignment (they were slated for a move)
5. Become pregnant with child number two

The husband reported on the results in a letter.

"Our car replacement came in June, completely beyond
any expectations. Regular play time with David
has become a reality and a joy. The people in our Bible
studies gave us money for Christmas for a really
nice sewing machine, which God gave us on sale. Our
assignment for the next year turned out to be a
fifth year at the same job, and we are excited about it.
And we are looking forward to the arrival of our
second child in January."

MAKING A LIST OF YOUR NEEDS OR DESIRES REQUIRES THAT YOU MAKE SOME DECISIONS.

You can't make a list of your needs without coming to
some decisions about them. If you're miserable in
your job, you still can't write something down to present

to God until you've decided just what it is you really want to have happen. Do you want your own attitude changed about your present job? Do you want a new job? Are you seeing that even another job like the one you have won't satisfy you and that what you really want is to change fields?

Making any such decision is hard work. It requires that you forsake those vague, restless feelings, leave behind all that griping-over-dinner to your wife about the boss, and move on out into what it is you really desire. But it's that decision that will activate your faith and bring it to life.

The book of 1 Samuel tells the story of the giant Goliath and the entire Philistine army coming against Israel. Because the two armies were at a standoff the Philistines had demanded sort of a one-on-one competition to determine the victor of the battle; so every day Goliath would come out, dressed in his armor, and challenge Israel to send a man to fight him.

When David the shepherd boy came to the Israelite camp he heard Goliath's challenge. By the time David arrived, Goliath had been making daily appearances for well over a month. Surely among all of the armies of Israel, there was a man or two whose hearts had been stirred to anger by Goliath's defamation of God. And surely there was more than one man who had thought, "God is more powerful than a giant, and I know he can send one of us out there to defeat that big windbag."

But the difference between David and those wishful thinkers was that when David saw the need and got the facts, he reviewed how God had worked for him in the past, and made a decision. He "made a list" of his desires and recited the list to Goliath.

"This day the Lord will deliver you into my hand, and I will strike you down; and cut off your head; and I will give the dead bodies of the host of the Philistines this day to the birds of the air and to the wild

beasts of the earth; that all the earth may know there is a
God in Israel" (1 Samuel 17:46). His list included
five requests, and God answered every one, because
David was operating in the power of an activated faith in
the living God.

Even if your list of needs has only one item on it,
writing that item down helps you come to a decision that
you will look to God to meet the need. It opens the
door for your faith to come alive.

MAKING A LIST HELPS YOU
FOCUS ON GOD RATHER THAN ON YOUR NEEDS.

A cloud of gloom can settle over you if you have a lot of
needs that are not clearly defined in your mind. They
can cloud your vision of God and create an atmosphere in
which doubt and fear thrive.

The answer to that gloom is to "... make plans,
counting on God to direct us" (Proverbs 16:9, TLB). Write
those needs down. Don't just write "money" if you
need $250 to pay a dental bill by July 17. Write $250 and
the July deadline. And if you're concerned about
your church, don't put down "Bless our church" if the
need is really that God silence the two couples who
are criticizing the pastor behind his back. Getting these
"plans made"—putting these needs down in writing—
frees you to count on God's direction and help and
provision. It gives a focus to your faith.

MAKING A LIST
OPENS YOUR EYES TO SEE GOD AT WORK.

I wasn't the first one to think of clarifying your needs.
Nehemiah came up with the idea centuries ago,
according to Scripture. The Bible tells that the king of
Assyria noticed that his Jewish servant Nehemiah
was looking a bit down and asked him the trouble.
Nehemiah responded honestly that he was discouraged
about his home city of Jerusalem lying in ruins.

And the king asked, "For what do you make request?" (Nehemiah 2:4).

Nehemiah came back with a specific, detailed answer right on the spot. I can just see him pulling a scroll out of his tunic and saying, "Now that you've asked..." He wanted to be sent back to Israel to do the rebuilding. He asked for letters of permission to pass safely through the countries on the way to Judah. And he wanted timber from the king's forest for the rebuilding.

Where do you suppose Nehemiah came up with such a quick answer? Look back one chapter. He'd just spent an extended time going over the situation with *the Lord*, and it was probably there that he, by faith, made the list and did the thinking necessary to determine what would be involved in rebuilding the city. So when the king asked to help, Nehemiah saw God's hand moving, and he was ready to reply.

Your faith list will open your eyes to see God at work when the provision comes by the hand of God.

MAKE SURE YOUR LIST ISN'T EDITED.

When you're writing down your needs and desires, do not edit them. Do not exclude some because they sound silly, selfish, materialistic, or unrealistic. Editing is God's job, not yours.

A college wrestler went up to talk to a speaker about the challenge to pray about everything.

"Here's the problem," the wrestler confided. "I'm working out with the goal of being the best wrestler in my weight class in the United States. But I just don't feel like I could or should pray about something like that."

The speaker didn't hesitate. "But *God* says you're to pray about everything," he declared flatly, referring the wrestler to Philippians 4:6. "There's no way

you can pray about everything and yet not pray about
that wrestling goal."

A couple of days later the wrestler was back. "I just
wanted to tell you that I have started praying
about my goal. I still want to be a top wrestler, but now
I have a new goal: I want to do it to the glory of God."

Because John 3:16 is such a tremendous focus of
the Christian faith, it's easy to miss a significant teaching
that follows in verses 20 and 21. Those two verses say:
"For every one who does evil hates the light, and
does not come to the light, lest his deeds should be
exposed. But he who does what is true comes to the light,
that it may be clearly seen that his deeds have
been wrought in God."

How do you know if your desire for a new Buick is from
God or not? You don't, and God doesn't expect you
to know. He wants you to take that desire for a Buick and
put it on your list of needs and desires—bring it
to the light—and then let God determine whether your
desire is right or not. You'll get nothing but frustration
if you try to determine whether or not to bring a
desire to God because you're not sure it's a "real need."
You're trying to do God's job, and frankly, you're
just not qualified. Let God edit your list once you have
put it down.

HOW TO OPEN YOUR LIST TO GOD
Start by praying over the things on your list and one of
five steps will follow:

1. *If you pray and get an answer, stop praying and thank
God.* In 1 Samuel 12, David prayed, wept, and fasted,
asking God for the life of his first child by Bathsheba, but
the child died. David's servants were afraid to tell
him, because they assumed that if he were so distraught
thinking that the child was merely sick, he'd probably

react violently to the news of his death. But instead, David got up, changed clothes, and went to worship God. He'd prayed, so when the answer came, he stopped praying and thanked God, and then went on to other concerns.

2. *If you pray and then some idea on your list seems dumb or you get a continued uneasiness in your heart about it, stop praying and scratch it off the list. God is saying no or beginning to lead you to an alternative.*

One lady wrote as her request: "A larger house for our family." After praying, she realized that it was the right request but wrong timing, so she scratched it. The bottom dropped out of another man's income the previous year, and he wrote that he would like his income to go up $6,000 the next year. But afterwards he said, "Every time I prayed that prayer, what came to my mind was: 'wrong number.' So I started to think: 'Probably too high.' Yet, when I started thinking and praying about $7,000, I had peace. So I continued to pray that way."

3. *If you pray and your heart continues to be burdened about the matter, keep on praying. God is leading.*

John Denver is one of the biggest names around in popular music today. But music was not the field he was heading into when he left high school and enrolled in architecture at Texas Tech.

"I tried to give myself to my studies," he told a reporter recently, "but music kept intruding. So I opted to go see if I could realize that dream inside of me. I was twenty. I felt I had time enough either to make it work or to get it out of my system and then become serious about my studies."

God may be leading you to similar experimentation with a need or desire of yours. As you pray, if you find that God continues to burden you about your dream, keep praying and assume that he is in it.

4. *If you pray and get peace, stop praying. The answer will come in God's timing.*

5. *If you've prayed for some time and you still get no answer, stop and evaluate.* Maybe your prayer needs to be more specific. Maybe God isn't answering because you haven't specified just what you want him to do, or maybe you need to ask for a particular timing, to tell God when you'd like it done.

I remember an incident on one of my first jobs after college, where I was supervising a lawn-care crew at the headquarters of a Christian organization. Work wasn't progressing because we needed a new mower. We'd prayed about it, but nothing was happening, until one morning when a young Christian who had just joined the crew began to pray. "Lord," he said, "those weeds are getting higher and higher, and they look bad. We can't do anything about it until we get that mower, so send it *this week*." By the end of the week, we had the mower.

God is a Giver with unlimited resources which he longs to share with you. The faith you need to start receiving those resources will come alive as you give your faith a focus. Sit down and make a list of your needs and desires. Make it specific and make it complete, then open it to God and let him edit it and fulfill it so you can start seeing your faith come alive.

FOUR
PRAYER: THE SAFE
AND POWERFUL WAY

*And whatever you ask in prayer you will receive, if you
have faith* (Matthew 21:22).

Since I've started working with people on how to live
by faith, I've heard the most interesting teachings on
prayer you could imagine. It's hard to do much by
faith without including prayer, so this topic comes up a
lot. And maybe someday I'll write a book like Art
Linkletter's *Kids Say the Darnedest Things*—except that
mine will be a compilation of the weird prayer
"doctrines" people come up with.

One man told me, "Anyone who prays more than once
about any request is doubting—he's not praying
in faith." I wondered how he matched that notion with
Jesus' command to be persistent in prayer.

A dear lady said to me, "I have a need and I'm really
praying *hard* about it." I thought to myself, "Why
not just pray believing? It's sure easier."

Which all goes to show that it's important to base your
guidelines for praying on the Word of God. It only
makes sense that if God is the One you talk with in your
prayers, and the One from whom you expect answers,

then you'd be wise to do that talking and asking
within the guidelines he's already provided for you. So
let's look at three Bible directives for praying in
faith and getting answers from God.

PRAY ABOUT EVERYTHING.

I'm sure that long before you reached high school
somebody passed on to you this piece of sage advice:
"NEVER say 'never.' " Or you may have learned the
hard way that just as soon as you say, "Everybody
knows that..." or "It always works to ... ," some smart
aleck will come along and prove you wrong. And in
light of all this, I've wondered if God knew the chance he
was taking when he issued the command in Philippians
4:6, TLB: "Don't worry about *anything*; instead, pray
about *everything* ..."

Everything??

A key punch operator who heard this statement from
Scripture responded as most of us probably do
subconsciously. "It can't mean *everything*! Some things
aren't spiritual enough to be prayed about, and
other things are too insignificant to bother God with."

Maybe that's what went through King Ahaz's mind
when the Lord gave him a Philippians 4:6 kind of
command. "Ask me for a sign, Ahaz, to prove that I will
indeed crush your enemies as I have said. Ask anything
you like, in heaven or on earth" (Isaiah 7:11, TLB).

"But the king," the story goes on, *"refused."*

He refused. Now that's what you'd call audacious. The
Lord of Heaven comes to him with a direct order,
and Ahaz says no. I wonder how Ahaz would have reacted
if one of his subjects had responded like that to
his commands.

Ahaz probably felt justified, however, because he had
what he saw as a "good" reason: "I'll not bother
the Lord with anything like that." A lady in a seminar told

me she tried to go all day long without asking God
for anything. Sounds awfully humble, doesn't it? But
according to God's response to Ahaz, he would have been
much more impressed with humility that showed
itself in obedience to his request.

"Then Isaiah said, O House of David, you aren't
satisfied to exhaust my patience; you exhaust the Lord's
as well!" (Isaiah 7:13, TLB).

It's interesting that the Lord rebuked Ahaz for not
asking, while nowhere in Scripture do we see anyone
rebuked for asking *too much*. Apparently God
means what he says when he tells you to pray about
everything. And "everything" includes all your physical,
emotional, and spiritual needs, as well as all those
things you are concerned about, and all your desires.

Most God-responsive people I know are enthusiastic
about praying for necessities like food or clothes or
housing or dental bills. They readily agree that everyone
should bring his or her concerns to the Lord in
prayer: worries about others' health and salvation and
much more. But they often get a little nervous when
the Word of God begins talking about asking God to give
them their desires. Somehow that just seems too
unspiritual.

A couple really raked me over the coals after I'd shared
the teaching of Psalm 37:4: "Be delighted with the
Lord. Then he will give you all your heart's desires"
(TLB). "Russ," they protested, "we pray about our
needs, and we pray about our concerns, but we would
never pray about our desires." People seem to
think such praying leads to being selfish, greedy, and
using God to get where we want to go. But I've
observed that often people who have this philosophy of
not bringing their desires to God seem to have a
very comfortable lifestyle, with many extras. So I've
concluded that they must pray about their needs
and their concerns, and then go out and buy their desires.

The problem with that philosophy is that if you don't pray, *you* get the credit for providing, instead of God. As I see it, God has not commanded us to do without our wants; he has told us not to be *controlled* by our wants. And by giving us many of those wants, he shows himself to be the generous Father that he is.

A group of Christian women in Kansas City were discussing a Bible passage which gives a bleak picture of what we often do instead of praying. The verse was: "You desire and do not have; so you kill. And you covet and cannot obtain; so you fight and wage war" (James 4:2). They concluded that none of them had killed anyone or started any war to get what they wanted, but their list of "what we do instead of praying" looked something like this: one nagged her husband; another complained a lot; another criticized those who had what she wanted; one worried; one had taken on a very time-consuming job; another put on a big garage sale. How's that for a updated version of James 4:2?

Why pray about everything? Do it because praying opens you up to God in whatever area you are coming to him. And that opening up allows him to enter your current situation to purify your motives and to give you *his* perspective. As 1 John 1:7 says, "If we walk in the light, as he is in the light, we have fellowship with one another, and the blood of Jesus his Son cleanses us from all sin." Living in the light isn't hard. It just means keeping your life open to God, so he's free to put his finger on anything that displeases him, and to share his burdens with you. The "how to" of that openness with God is to pray about everything.

REMEMBER WHAT YOU'VE PRAYED.
Maybe in Sunday school you heard the story of Gideon putting out a fleece to get a confirmation of God's

leading to him. He was frightened about what God had just told him to do. So, to get a special *yes* that God was with him, he laid a sheepskin out on the ground one night, and asked the Lord to make the sheepskin wet and the ground dry, as a sign of God's being with him. And the next morning that's just what had happened.

Can you imagine the confusion that would have resulted if Gideon had prayed but had not remembered just how he'd worded the request? "Let's see, here," he'd have mused, "did I say the ground should be wet, and the sheepskin dry, or the skin wet and the ground dry?" And he'd call to his wife, "Honey, how was it again that we prayed about this sheepskin thing?" He might have missed the whole message from God!

In Mark 11:23, God gives you a tremendous amount of authority. It says, in effect, that you'll have what you pray, whatever you say.

During the time I was selling real estate, a moratorium was put on new gas hook-ups in the Colorado Springs area. As a result, exchanges ground to a halt. I had only one listing in three months, and believe me, that's no way to keep your family in hot dogs, so I began to wonder if the Lord was telling me I should get out of real estate. I wasn't sure of his will, so I prayed this way: "Lord, I'll tentatively make this my last month of selling real estate. And if you bless it and I do well, I'll take that as a sign you want me to quit. But if you don't bless it, I'll stay in."

That month, things went wild. During those thirty days, my sales totalled 50 percent more than I'd sold in the last *year*. So I told my boss I was quitting.

"Quitting!" he exploded. "You've just started going well here. Why would you want to quit now?" So I explained about what I prayed.

"Are you sure you didn't get it wrong?" he pressed me. "I mean, I could see you quitting if you had continued

to do poorly, but all this selling surely means you're to
stay in the business. Anyone could see that!"

But that wasn't how I'd prayed.

So *remember* what you pray. Write it down, if you need
to, because later the situation may look different
to you and you may misinterpret what God is doing.

A lady in one of my seminars told me how glad she was
she'd written down her request to God that she be
expecting another child by November. "Some
circumstances have changed for us since I prayed," she
told me, "and if I hadn't remembered that this baby
is an answer to prayer, I'm not sure how excited I'd be
about it right now."

Another young couple I met told me about how they'd
prayed that God would give them a ministry with
engaged couples to help prepare them for marriage, but
nothing happened for a while, and they forgot the
request. Later, their church was filling positions in the
Sunday school, and they were asked to help with the
single adult class.

"We were both a little disappointed," the wife confided,
"because we knew a teacher in the young couples
class was leaving, and that's the job we really wanted.
We'd gotten to know some of the people in that
department, and were excited about serving there. But
the offer we got instead was for this singles class."

But their disappointment left when they realized that
God was just answering their prayer of months
before. In the singles class were three engaged couples,
and of course the potential for several more. They
started a special Bible study with these couples, and saw
God fulfill them in it.

When the angel came to Daniel after he'd prayed about
Israel's being freed from captivity, he told Daniel,
"I have come because of your words" (Daniel 10:12).
So remember what those words are, or you'll perhaps
miss the answers when they come.

PRAY SPECIFICALLY.

Suppose you were the angel Gabriel and God made you
responsible for sorting the requests that come to
heaven for answers. Would you know how to answer *your*
kind of prayers? What would you do, for instance,
with those requests to "bless Aunt Jane"? Are your
requests so general that when you get an answer
you can hardly recognize it? What does a "blessing" look
like, anyway?

A working girl in a seminar on faith wrote down on a
Sunday night that she wanted God to give her a
new car. Hers had a bashed-in side, and it was time for a
new one. On Monday her boss called her into his
office. "We want you to go over to the Ford dealership,"
he said, "and pick up a new lease car for your use.
We've decided that with the work you're doing for us, you
should have a company car."

When she reported back to the faith seminar on
Monday evening she stood up and asked, "Can I change
my order?"

I asked what she meant. "What I really wanted was a
Chevy," she replied, "and God gave me a Ford."

"Too bad," I told her. "If you wanted a Chevy, you
should have asked for one. How is God supposed to know
if you just send up a general order for a new car?
He probably figured any new car would do since you
didn't get specific. Next time, if you want a Chevy, ask for
a Chevy."

At the end of one of the sessions in Massachusetts, a
fellow let me know in very firm words that you
could not ask God to do things in detail. But that night, he
came back to the meeting, put his arm around me
and said, "I need to apologize to you because this
afternoon I went home and looked up all those verses that
were shared this morning. I had to conclude that
the Bible does tell us to be specific."

The man in Luke 11 got specific when he had friends

stop unexpectedly for the night. It was midnight, and
the 7-11 store had closed, so he went next door
and asked his neighbor for three loaves of bread. Notice
he didn't just ask for "bread." He was probably
figuring that they'd want a snack before they went to bed
(that's one loaf) and toast for breakfast (that's two).
And he'd need a third to make sandwiches they could take
with them when they left in the morning. He asked
for three and he got three. Most people would probably
just ask for bread, wind up with two loaves, and
then have to make open-faced sandwiches for lunch
because they were short.

A woman I met in Africa came storming up to me after
a message on living on faith. "I just want you to
know," she fumed, "that there are limits on this believing
God stuff. My daughter is getting married, and really
needs a house, but all we could pray for is a room. She
can't get a house because of the color of her skin."

I looked at her a minute. "You said she needs a house.
What did you pray for?"

"We prayed for a room," she repeated.

God is bigger than a social system, bigger than man's
prejudice. If you need a house and you *pray* for a *house*,
then a house it will be.

A senior missionary who overheard the conversation
told me about an incident he was involved in in Africa
at the end of World War II. Racial lines were clearly
drawn then, too, in South Africa; and housing was
so short that there was a seven-year waiting list for the
available houses.

It was during this time that a colored (the mixed race
in South Africa) alcoholic came to know Christ at
a Christian conference. Before the conference was over,
God revealed to the alcoholic that he had a house
for him in a particular subdivision, so the man went
around announcing it to everyone at the conference. No
one encouraged him much, though, because they

knew it was unlikely that he'd get a house—and in that particular subdivision, they knew it was impossible.

When he came home from the conference, he went to see the woman responsible for "his" subdivision, and said, "God has told me you have a house for me here."

The woman laughed. "He hasn't told me anything like that, so you'd better get your message a little clearer!"

But the man was undaunted.

"Are you on our waiting list?" she asked him. He wasn't.

She stopped a minute and looked at him. "What I want to know is," she said, "how did you find out about the house we have available? This past weekend is the first time in I don't know how long that we've had any houses to be occupied. How did you find out? We've kept it secret."

The man insisted he hadn't "found out" anywhere, but God had told him there was a house for him there. And he told the woman about his conversion that weekend, and his desire to give his family something better than he had given them during all of his lifetime.

The woman listened and finally shook her head. "I don't know what to think about what you're saying, and I don't know why I'm doing this, but the house is yours." And he left with the keys.

If you need a house, pray for a house. Pray specifically and God will answer specifically, no matter what the barriers.

A girl I met at a Christian conference told me she'd applied the "pray specifically" principle to her love life, with some interesting results. Because she'd been hurt in several relationships already, she asked God to never let her get emotionally involved with a man unless he was the one she was to spend her life with. And she asked God to show her who that "one" would be by having him send her roses. This was all back in 1973.

Three years later she met Don. She was dating another fellow at the time, but she and Don became friends,

and for no apparent reason, Don sent her roses.
Remembering her prayer, Sharon got a little shaky. So
she prayed again, "Look, God, maybe this is just
nothing. Maybe you don't remember what I prayed about
the one who sends me roses being *the one*. If it's
really Don, let him give me flowers again—but it doesn't
have to be roses this time."

A week later, Don was taking Sharon out to dinner.
On the way to meet her, he stopped to pay his florist bill
—and decided to take her a rose corsage as a surprise.

Sharon said, "I never told him what I'd prayed. It even
terrified me! But six months later we started talking
about marriage." They're Mr. and Mrs. today.

Another single girl at the conference decided to pray
about romance too, and put on her faith list: "That
I could go to the couples conference next year."

The next year she did go, but not as she'd expected.
That year, the singles conference as such was cancelled
and combined with a couples conference. She concluded,
"I just wasn't specific enough with God. I asked
to go to the couples conference—and that's what God
gave me. What I really wanted was to be *married* and
going to that conference! Next time I'm going to make
it clear!"

God will give you what you ask for.

DON'T BE AFRAID
YOU'RE PRAYING OUT OF GOD'S WILL.

I've met Christians who are afraid to pray about
everything because they fear they'll ask for something
that God doesn't want them to have; God will give it,
and they'll be stuck in a big mess. If this sounds like you,
fear no more. Prayer is the safe and powerful way.

If you ask "amiss"—for a car God doesn't want you to
have or a job he never intended for you—relax.
God will not zap you, or put you on the shelf, or remove
his hand from your life. He just won't give you what
you ask for. Could that be more simple?

That's what James 4:3 promises. This verse relates to
when you "ask wrongly, to spend it on your passions."
Now that's not a good motive. It's asking for a Cadillac
solely to impress the neighbors. Or asking that
the Sunday school class you teach grows, just so everyone
will know what a terrific teacher you are. And if you
pray like that, here's what God says: "You ask, and
do not receive."

The Holy Spirit's job is to intercede for you in prayer
—that's what Romans 8 makes clear. So if your
motives are bad, he'll sort through it all and see to it that
you don't get the things that would be harmful to you.
But don't try to do what only the Holy Spirit is
equipped to do. If you know you're praying for a
particular thing out of a rotten motivation, please stop;
but if you're not sure of your motive, go ahead
and pray. You're safe, because if your motive is wrong, or
if it would be bad for you, or out of God's will, God
just won't give it to you. You're completely protected.

A word of caution. If you decide to go ahead and
act *without* praying, God will probably let you. When the
children of Israel complained in the wilderness,
longing for meat after God had already provided all they
needed in the form of manna, God answered their
request with quail. But he also gave them "leanness to
their soul." Keep in mind that this was not the prayer of a
people seeking the Lord. They were entirely bent on
their own way, and if God hadn't answered their prayers,
they'd have figured out a way to answer it themselves.

Don't let getting out of God's will keep you from
praying. God will protect you if you keep your life all
open to him by praying about everything.

Living by faith. Most of it happens as you learn to
pray—praying about everything, praying specifically,
and remembering what you've asked God to do.
Prayer is the safe and powerful way to live by faith.

FIVE
RECEIVING
IN THE WILL OF GOD

*Therefore do not be foolish, but understand what the
Lord's will is* (Ephesians 5:17).

I know of a church with elective Sunday school classes,
where the adults choose a new study topic every
three months. The pastor told me that if they can have
someone teach on how to know God's will, they can
run that same class over and over because they'll always
have people signing up for it.

That doesn't surprise me. I've spoken in a lot of
Christian conferences where part of the afternoon is set
aside for workshops on how-to's of Christian living.
Invariably, if one of the workshops is "Knowing the Will
of God," half the people sign up for it, even if there
are ten other choices.

All of this tells me two things: people want to know
God's will, and they're confused about it. It was probably
to this confusion that the Apostle Paul was speaking
when he said, "Therefore do not be foolish, but
understand what the Lord's will is" (Ephesians 5:17). And
when God says, "Understand what the Lord's will is,"
that's a command. It means that if you want to

pick something to devote your energy to, being wise about God's will is a good place to invest.

Three concepts are basic to understanding God's will. If all three are a part of your life, they'll answer a lot of the day-to-day questions that come up about "I wonder if God wants me to..." First, you need to *be committed to doing* God's will. And second, you have to *realize God is already working in you*. Third, you have to *launch out*.

COMMIT YOURSELF TO DOING GOD'S WILL.
Imagine this. You've got mother-in-law problems, and you're tearing your hair out trying to figure out how to solve them. So, in desperation, you decide to become one of the millions of Americans who write to Ann Landers for advice. You spell out the whole problem, and then close with, "Okay, Ann, what shall I do?"

A week later you get a registered letter with "Ann Landers" on the return. You rip it open, and here's what she says. "You did the right thing in writing to me about your mother-in-law because I've been involved in several situations like yours, and I know exactly what to do. The solution I have will completely change your situation for the better, and you'll never have to worry about it again. I've seen it work dozens of times, even in problems much more complex than yours.

"There's just one thing. I'll tell you the answer as soon as you give me your signed statement that you'll follow what I say, no matter what I ask of you."

Now what? You grab another piece of paper and start to fire off a letter to Ann, agreeing that you'll do whatever she says. But then you stop. Who knows what she's going to suggest? What if it involves selling your house, quitting your job, and moving to another state? What if it involves killing your mother-in-law? She did say, "No matter what I ask of you." What if...?

If this were Ann Lander's policy, she'd be operating on the same premise God does with his children, because he does not reveal his will to curiosity seekers.
You can't come to him saying, "Tell me what you want for me, and then I'll decide whether I want to do it."
What God asks of you is to sign a contract without the terms of the deal filled in. He asks for a commitment to do what he says before he reveals what that is.

That's what Jesus was teaching when he said, "If a man chooses to do God's will, he will find out whether my teaching comes from God or whether I speak on my own" (John 7:17, NIV). If you're willing to do, then you'll know. If you stacked up all the verses in the Bible on *doing* the will of God in one pile, and the verses on *knowing* the will of God in another, you'd have a giant pile on doing, and a skinny little stack on knowing. Once you're committed to the doing, the knowing comes easy.

You may be more like the guy who was in love with two girls at once, and couldn't decide which one to marry. He decided he'd better ask God's help, so he prayed, "God, I'll flip a coin, and you direct it: heads it's Jane; tails it's Judy." He flipped a quarter, looked at it, saw it had come up tails, and said, "Okay, God how about two out of three?"

You won't know until you're willing to do.

Does that sound scary? Does something inside you cringe at the idea of an unconditional commitment to God's choices for you? Maybe you've never said it in so many words, but inside you're thinking, "If I tell God I'll do *anything*, he'll send me out to be a little green shriveled-up missionary in Africa." Or "The wife he'll pick for me will probably be a parolee from the Louisiana State School for the Ugly."

If that's what you feel, then you're listening to exactly the same line the devil has been using with God's children since the Garden of Eden. When Eve told the

serpent that God wouldn't let them eat from the
tree of good and evil, Satan had a ready comeback. "You
will not die. For God knows that when you eat of it
your eyes will be opened, and you will be like God,
knowing good and evil" (Genesis 3:4, 5).

Lie Number One: What God says is not true. God had
said they *would* die, and Satan turned right
around and said they wouldn't.

Lie Number Two: God's decisions are not for your best.
Satan said God didn't want them to eat the fruit
because he didn't want any competition in the wisdom
department; he wanted all the power for himself.

Now listen to this. "I know the plans I have for you,
says the Lord, plans for welfare and not for evil,
to give you a future and a hope" (Jeremiah 29:11). And he
declares in Romans 12:2 that his will is good, acceptable,
and perfect. God's choices for you are the very
best ones that could be made, because he knows you and
he can look over all the possible options, to select
the one from the thousands that fits the best. And that's
something you can't do for yourself. You could
probably come up with some decisions that were good,
like doing well in your job. And you could probably make
some choices that were pleasing, like stopping at
Baskin Robbins for a Rocky Road sundae. But you don't
have the capacity to make for yourself *perfect*
choices, because as a human being you can't see all the
available alternatives. The job you choose on your
own might be the closest-to-perfect one you could find
right now, but how do you know that in some other
place there is not a job that would suit you even better?

God can promise that his choices for you will be
perfect because he knows all the options, and because the
goodness of his choices is based on the kindness of
his character and on the reliability of his Word. Don't be
afraid to give God a free hand in leading you. If

you're going to be afraid, fear only choosing to listen to
the devil's lies about God.

HOW TO KNOW
WHETHER YOU'RE COMMITTED TO GOD'S WILL.

Imagine for a moment that you are Moneybags Malone
and everybody knows it. A friend comes to ask you
if he can borrow $1,000. He makes a good case, sounds
sincere, and promises to pay you back. But this
is the same guy who promised he'd pay you for the NFL
game tickets you picked up for him. And he promised
he'd take care of the dent he put in your car the last time
he borrowed it. Your fender is still bent, and it
looks as if the tickets were on you. So how much weight
does his word on repaying the $1,000 hold?

Don't be too hard on the poor guy. Isn't that just how
we appear to God when we make those "I'll choose
any career you want me to" kind of commitments, yet we
say our twelve-year-old is really only ten when
it comes time to pay for his theatre ticket? God is not as
concerned about where you live or what you do for a
living as he is about what you *are*. Paul wrote: "Whether
you eat or drink or *whatever* you do, do all to the
glory of God" (1 Corinthians 10:31). It doesn't matter to
God so much what you do as what you are in the midst
of your doing. If you specialize on being the kind of person
God wants you to be, he will lead you into activities,
careers, and locations he has planned for you.

In the list of people God honored in Hebrews 11, only
Samuel was a preacher. There are farmers, kings,
shepherds, and even a prostitute, but only one preacher,
and he was asleep when he was called. God checks
the character of people, and when they are obeying
day-by-day his obvious commands for them, then he is
free to trust them with his leading.

So when you start asking yourself, "Am I willing to do

God's will in this big decision?"—back up! Ask
another question first. "Am I *now* doing what I know God
wants for me?" Jesus said, "If you are offering
your gift at the altar, and there remember that your
brother has something against you, leave your gift there
before the altar. First go and be reconciled to your
brother; then come and offer your gift" (Matthew
5:23, 24, NIV).

What does God want for you? It's easy to figure out.
He wants you to be kind to your spouse and kids
and the people at work and the grouch next door; he wants
you to be honest; he wants you to stay open to him.
His will for you is do-able. And as you do it on a day-to-day
basis, those climactic periods of struggling over a
commitment to him will become easier and easier.

Knowing God's will starts with commitment to do what
he says.

BELIEVE THAT GOD IS WORKING WITHIN YOU.
"It is God who works in you to will and to act according
to his good purpose" (Philippians 2:13, NIV). If
you're committed to doing the will of God, you should
expect that your knowledge of his will, will not come to
you out of a vacuum. God is already working *in you*.
Some of the believers I meet seem to think that
after they commit themselves to doing God's will, they
will have to grab hold of God and try to squeeze
his will out of him. That is an erroneous idea. If you've
given yourself to him, God will be revealing his will
to you all the time. It's simply a matter of recognizing
how he does it.

One of the most obvious ways in which God is at work
inside you is through his Word. Maybe the issues
you're grappling with are not really issues at all, like
whether or not you should provide for your family,
and whether or not you should be helping others find

Christ. These issues are clearly dealt with in the Word; you can go right ahead and do them with no hassle about whether he wants you to or not.

A businessman in Kansas City told me about a new job he'd applied for. It offered an outstanding position that would have helped him finally measure up to his father's ideas of success for him; at the same time, it would have demanded a great amount of time away from his family, and it would have removed some real opportunities for Christian growth. He struggled with the decision, but after understanding God's perspective on the responsibility he had to his family, and on the need to keep growing as a Christian, he told God he'd do whatever he said.

"I completely forgot about the interviews until I was called in to give the company an answer," he told me. "Suddenly I heard myself saying no, and I felt a flood of relief because I'd received peace instead of a position."

A woman told me how frustrated she was because her job demanded so much time, and she had begun to realize that God wanted her to spend more time with her husband. "But I need the job," she told me, "to make our house payment."

I asked her how long she'd been married, and she told me six months. When I heard that, I agreed with her that she did probably need to be spending more time with her husband.

"Why don't you go ahead and quit the job so you can be with your husband," I suggested, "and let God make your house payment?" It didn't take a prophet to come up with that insight, since the Scriptures had already made the priority of her marriage clear.

One of the chief ways God works in you to direct you is through his Word.

Another way the Lord can prompt you is by your *hearing a need*. World Vision International was born because Bob Pierce took a trip to the Far East

after World War II and saw the tremendous needs there.
From that awareness came an organization that
reaches out to physical and spiritual needs of millions.
I heard not long ago that some 500 Christian movements
now in existence all came into being after World
War II. The impetus for many of them came largely from
American servicemen who, while stationed in Europe
and the Pacific, saw with their own eyes tremendously
needy people without Christ. When you see or hear
of a need, be alert. God may be directing you.

There's another way God is at work within you—a way
that doesn't get much credit these days. That way
is through the use of *your brain*. Dawson Trotman,
founder of the Navigators, used to say, "The Lord
gave you a lot of leading when he gave you a brain."

If you're faced with a decision, make up a list of
the alternatives and think through the consequences of
each choice. "Seek and you will find," says Luke 11:9, and
I think this has to do with seeking information when
you must make a decision.

Solomon advised, "By wise counsel thou shalt make thy
war: and in multitude of counsellors there is safety"
(Proverbs 24:6, KJV). Information can be a tremendous
safety factor in figuring out what God wants for
you, because at first glance almost every opportunity you
come across looks golden. If you're disgruntled,
or if you don't like your present job, or if you don't like
your brand of Christianity, the grass looks awfully
green on the other side of the fence.

Any opportunity that comes up will look like a real
peach to you. But you must remember what's inside
all peaches: *pits!* Investigate those pits so you won't
become surprised when you bite into the fruit. Seek
a balance of information. Get both sides of each story.

Seek information from people who have what you
need to know. Go to the person who is doing what you
want to do. I wouldn't ask the most successful

businessman in town to advise me on growing spiritually if he himself is not growing. Nor would I ask a pastor for advice about going into business if he's never done anything like that. Figure out who has the best information and go to those people.

Don't think that getting information cancels out God's role. Solomon said, "Trust in the Lord with all your heart, and do not rely on your own insight" (Proverbs 3:5). Here the word *rely* is translated from the Hebrew word that means *to support one's self*. So don't support yourself with (make decisions based on) your own insight alone. Give God the decision-making role, because he'll close the door you choose if he wants to.

If you realize that God is at work within you, you'll see him working to lead you through his Word and through the needs you hear about, and also through your use of your own brain. But he also uses *your desires*.

Have you ever thought, "I sure wouldn't mind spending a month in Europe"? Or "It would be a good experience for my family to live three months on a mission field to see what it's like"? What did you do with those thoughts? Did you write them off at once as ridiculous and impractical?

I talked with a certain member of my Sunday school class about substituting for me as the class teacher for the next few weeks, but he turned me down. "Two years ago," he explained, "my wife and I started thinking about things we'd really like to do. At that time I told both her and God that I'd really like to become a college teacher."

With his particular set of circumstances at that time, his dream seemed like a dumb idea. But instead of dismissing it, he prayed about it and decided that God was using that desire to lead him. So he started taking a couple of classes at the community college and before long, the college administration discovered that he had real teaching ability. He's taking only one course now;

he's *teaching* the other one! And from that beginning, God opened up other opportunities for him.

Your desires may in reality be God at work in you to direct you.

A big part of knowing God's will is already going on inside you. You just need to become aware of his Spirit already at work with your spirit to direct you: through his Word, through the needs you hear of, or through your own thoughts or desires. If you're committed to doing his will, and if you're responsive to his work in you, then you're ready for the next step: *Launch out.*

LAUNCH OUT.
You've done all the finding out you need for now. You won't know more about God's will until you move out. Here's my formula for launching: P-P-P/A-S-K. It's two ways of saying the same thing. Matthew 7:7, 8 tells you to ask, seek, and knock (A-S-K). I translate those three as Pray, Peace, Press (P-P-P).

Start by *praying*. Tell God you want to do his will, not yours, and ask him to guide you.

Then determine whether you have *peace*. Paul said, "Let the peace of Christ rule in your hearts" (Colossians 3:15, NIV). That means God's peace is to be the *umpire* in your heart. It's the umpire's job to decide if the play or the pitch was right or not. So let God's peace say yes or no. If you don't have peace, back off. But if you do, move on.

Once you've prayed and have peace, then *press ahead*. Go ahead and try it—it might be right! That's what Paul did and he explained: "One thing I do: Forgetting what is behind and straining toward what is ahead, I press on toward the goal to win the prize for which God has called me" (Philippians 3:13, 14, NIV).

When you do launch out, one of two things will happen. The door may open up, and the resources you need

to do the job will be supplied for you. Or else the door
will close and you can say, "Thanks, God. I guess
it was not your will after all."

Remember that when God closes a door, that's his
leading: it's not a lack of leading. So if you've told people
what your plan is, and then God closes the door, just
smile and say, "It was not the will of God." The only thing
that will be hurt is your pride, and pride is no great
virtue to cultivate anyway.

Don't be afraid to launch out. There's no need to fear
that some evil consequence will come if you make
a decision that you mistakenly believed to be God's will
because God will not desert you. He'll be there to
pick up the pieces with you and to help you move again in
a new direction if you need to.

Launching out could be pretty scary if we didn't know
for sure that God is always watching out for us. So
just tell God, "If you have a file that you look through
whenever you think about me, please put a red card in
there to show that *I want to do your will*. No matter how
I may think at a given moment, and no matter what
trials or troubles come my way, there's one thing I want:
to be in your will." When you've communicated that
attitude to God, go ahead with confidence that he will
protect you.

GOD'S WILL AND THE UNEXPECTED.
What do you do when something surprising comes along
and upsets your well-balanced Christian life?

When you have initiated an intentional change in your
life circumstances, it's easy to feel secure. But
when an unexpected change takes place, it may throw you
if you aren't ready to handle it.

One day when I came home from work my wife told me
that our neighbor had been fired from his job. So I went to
their house after dinner, and I found depression
everywhere.

"Did you like the job?" I asked him.

"It's the best job—it *was* the best job I ever had," he
moaned. "A couple of weeks ago another fellow was
talking about quitting. I thought to myself how dumb that
would be for me, because the company was growing
and I was growing with it. But the boss walked in today
and said I was fired—with hardly any explanation."

"Do you believe that all things work together for good
for those who love God?" I asked him.

He looked at me and answered slowly, "Yes, I guess so."

"Then God has allowed this to happen," I said. "And
the Bible says, 'In everything give thanks.' Even
though you don't know how this is all going to turn out,
you at least know it's God's will that you give thanks. So
every time you think about it tomorrow, say, 'Thanks,
God,' because he is allowing it to happen as part of his
good and perfect plan. If people ask you what happened,
tell them you got fired, but then tell them you
believe it's all part of God's perfect plan, and it's going
to work out for good."

The next day the neighbor's boss called to tell me how
amazed he was at the complete turn-around in this
man's attitude. He was actually thankful and rejoicing,
and the boss couldn't understand it. So I had to
explain it all to him.

When it was all over, my neighbor sold his house at a
nice profit, at a time when houses weren't selling well.
And the new job God gave him was far better in
experience value than the one from which he'd been fired.

God has a better plan for you than any boss,
professor, organization, or person, so accept the
unexpected with faith and thanksgiving. God is just
keeping you in his will.

As his child, God has given you the opportunity to live
your life in the center of his will. All you need to
do to turn that opportunity into reality is to be willing to
do his will, aware that he's at work in you, and then
launch out on what he's shown.

55

SIX
YOUR INVISIBLE
MEANS OF SUPPORT

Give and it will be given to you; good measure, pressed down, shaken together, running over (Luke 6:38).

I met Boet and Winnie Lewis when I was on a seven-week speaking tour in South Africa. Both in their early fifties, Boet and Winnie lived in government-subsidized housing that rented for $20 a month because Boet had been physically disabled in a car wreck. If I remember right, their total income from the government at that time was about $35 or $45 a month.

If I had heard about their situation before I'd met them, I probably would have visited with a full-of-pity attitude. But ten minutes with them convinced me that I was talking with people who needed no pity.

At forty-seven, Boet had led a tough life, including a lot of drinking, and people had encouraged Winnie to leave him because they said he was just no good and probably never would be. He couldn't hold a job and he faced (and caused) problem after problem. But that was before a missionary came to his home and introduced him to Jesus Christ. Then both his life and Winnie's changed dramatically.

As I sat in their living room, both were bubbling over with what God was doing for them. "I want you to know how much the Lord has been blessing us," Boet began. "See this new carpeting? We just spent $200 for it." And out front beside their car stood a two-year-old Mazda pickup. They also had a washing machine now, and some good furniture.

It didn't take an economist to figure out that that's pretty good on a $45-a-month check. I asked how it happened.

"It all started," Winnie explained, "because we were so low on finances. We didn't know what to do, so we decided together to start giving to God. I took a job that paid between $13 and $14 a week, and each week when that pay envelope came, we'd take part of it out before we did any bill paying, and give it to the Lord.

"Don't think that wasn't hard to do that first year, when I knew we needed that money so much. But we'd decided to give by faith, so we stuck to it."

A year later, God began to give back to them. They came up with the idea of starting a little business of their own, so Boet got licenses to deliver fruits, vegetables, and fish, and he started a delivery route. Through that delivery route the Lord gave them many of the other things they now own.

The Lord's doings prompted them to give more yet. Before I left Cape Town, Boet told me, "My wife and I have prayed about raising our giving, and I've decided to give $20 a month more than I had been. And Winnie has announced to me that I'll have to raise her wages $10 a month (she keeps my books) because the Lord has told her to give $10 a month more."

During the first month of their giving the increased amounts, God did a special thing for them. It was January, which is usually the poorest month of the year in

the fish business because many customers are gone
on holiday or are out of money because of Christmas
spending. But during that January, Boet made a hundred
dollars more than he had made in October, November,
and December. Figure that out, Mr. Businessman.

Many people just give and that's the end of it. Others,
like Boet and Winnie, give and find that God in
return gives and gives and gives back to them. What
makes the difference? I think it may be that the
non-getters make one of three mistakes—the "10
percent" mistake, or the "when we can afford it" mistake,
or the "God needs help" mistake.

TEN PERCENT—WHO SAID SO?

Somebody somewhere is propagating the idea that every
follower of Christ ought to be giving 10 percent of
his income, his time, his ability to God. And they say that
if you are giving 10 percent you are doing "biblical
giving." That somebody needs to recheck Scripture.

Nowhere in the New Testament do I find the idea that
God's calculator is locked in on 10 percent. I do see in the
New Testament these guidelines: ". . . as God has
prospered him" (1 Corinthians 16:2, KJV); "Freely ye
have received, freely give" (Matthew 10:8, KJV): and
". . . each one must do as he has made up his mind,
not reluctantly, or under compulsion" (2 Corinthians 9:7).
I see no percentage signs in there anywhere.

Now, it's true that the Old Testament law often used
percentage guidelines. A tenth of each person's
income was to go to the Levites who cared for the house of
God (Leviticus 27:30-33). But that wasn't all. In
addition, a second tithe was to pay for a sacred meal in
Jerusalem (Deuteronomy 12:5, 6). And every third
year, another tithe went for the Levites, strangers,

fatherless, and widows (Deuteronomy 14:28, 29). If you
want to talk percentages, the Old Testament standard
was closer to 23 percent of the people's income than
it was to 10.

Let God tell you what to give—don't use some standard
you heard somewhere.

After we'd had a session in one of the churches in South
Africa, suggesting that the people pray about how
much God would have them to give, one man could hardly
wait to speak up. "This morning," he reported, "I was
praying about what my wife and I should give to the
church, and the thought came to my mind that it should be
twenty rand. I walked into the bedroom, and there
was twenty rand lying on the dresser. I asked my wife
what the money was for, and she answered, 'God spoke
to me that we should increase our giving by that
much, so I just laid it out on the dresser so it would be
available.' "

A few nights later, we were in the home of a
businessman who shared how his spiritual life had really
been rejuvenated by giving. Years before, when he
had fallen away from the Lord, he had married a girl who
wasn't a Christian, and things were going badly for them.

"It was rough for us in a lot of ways," he told me.
"We couldn't pay our bills and were going in debt. We
couldn't buy even essentials, like furniture. So I
suggested to my wife that we start giving to the Lord.

"Since she wasn't a Christian it seemed like a pretty
crazy solution to the problems we were having, but
she told me that even though she didn't know anything
about it, if *I* knew, I should go ahead and try it. So we
started giving away 5 percent of our income.

"In just three months we were out of debt and starting
to buy furniture. Best of all, in that three months,
my wife came to know Christ as her Savior."

"Are you still giving 5 percent?" I asked.

He smiled. "We're way over the top of that now."

Don't be locked in on 10 percent.

GIVE YOUR FAITH
A PUSH BY GIVING FIRST.

A few weeks ago when I had lunch with a businessman in Colorado Springs, we hadn't even finished eating before he told me about his money troubles. Not only was he not making anything, he had just lost $5,000. Later in the conversation, he added that he was $4,000 behind in a commitment he'd made to give to others.

At the time, I didn't put those two pieces of information together, but a week later I thought about it and stopped in his office. "Listen, Jim," I said. "I think I can tell you why you lost money last year."

"You don't need to tell me, Russ," he responded. "I already know. We didn't give what we'd promised to the Lord *first*."

I pulled his *Living Bible* off the shelf, and together we read Proverbs 3:9, 10: "Honor the Lord by giving him the *first* part of all your income, and he will fill your barns with wheat and barley and overflow your wine vats with the finest wines."

As far as I can tell, one good reason why God thought up this idea of giving first to him is that it reminds us that everything we have is from him. He—not the paycheck—is the source of provision. Giving first to God is in line with Deuteronomy 8:18: "You shall remember the Lord your God: for it is he who gives you power to get wealth."

When Fred Krebs called me not long ago, he was excited. "The other night," he told me, "I was doing some thinking and I realized that God had been telling me we should give away $10 a month more than we had been. When I told my wife, she was positive, but reminded me that our utility bill wasn't paid and we didn't have enough money to give and pay the bill both."

It looked like a conflict, but they both agreed that if God had spoken, they'd better give—and trust him about the utility bill.

"So that night," Fred continued, "we sat down and

wrote out a check for $10 and gave it away. The very next day, we received $50 in the mail. And we gave away $5 of the $50. And the following day we received a $100 check in the mail as a gift to us. I'm wondering now how much we'd have gotten if we'd given more than $5 of the $50!"

If you're not getting, maybe you're not giving first.

IS GOD POOR AND IN NEED OF HELP?

Don't get the idea that God wants you to give because he needs your resources. Giving is not for his good—it's for yours. Remember when Jesus directed Peter to get tax money from the mouth of a fish? If God needs cash he can find a way to get it. He's not depending on you or me to keep him from starving or from closing down his operations.

GIVING IS A WAY TO GET TO KNOW GOD AS YOUR FATHER/PROVIDER.

God may not be getting enough chances to provide for you because you're taking care of your own needs instead of using your resources to care for the needs of others. God may be wanting to show you what a generous provider he can be, but you just aren't giving him a chance. By getting rid of some of your own resources you will be giving him room to work.

GIVING IS A WAY TO SEND TREASURE AHEAD TO HEAVEN.

You may have heard the imaginary account of a rich man who died and went to heaven. After he arrived, he was assigned an angel-guide who was to show him to his heavenly home. As they walked up the street, the angel said, "This huge house here belongs to the maid you had on earth." The rich man was impressed because the maid's place was fronted by huge pillars, and it had a four-car garage.

"And this one," the angel said as they moved farther up the street, "is your neighbor's house. Pretty nice, don't you think?"

They kept walking. Finally they stopped near a little corrugated tin shack about six by six, and the angel announced, "This one is yours."

The man groaned. "There must be a mistake. You saw my maid's house and my neighbor's. Surely they didn't wind up with those and I with this!"

"I checked the record," the angel replied, "and this is it. Maybe the problem is that you didn't understand how we operate up here. We build with the material you send up while you're on earth, and this is all you sent."

Though you can't use that story as the basis for a doctrinal statement, I do like the way it illustrates the heart of what Jesus was trying to communicate in Matthew 6:19-21 KJV: "Lay not up for yourselves treasures upon earth, where moth and rust doth corrupt, and where thieves break through and steal; but lay up for yourselves treasures in heaven, where neither moth nor rust doth corrupt, and where thieves do not break through nor steal, for where your treasure is, there will your heart be also."

GOD WANTS YOU TO GIVE SO YOU'LL GET.

I remember talking about giving in a Sunday night church service in which they later took up an offering. After the service a missionary came up to talk with me. "You know," he said, "this really works! My wife and I gave $13 in the offering, and we've already gotten back $13.13."

And at ten that night a pastor called me with an exciting story. "I was sitting in church tonight," he said, "and all I had was two dollars and sixty cents. So I decided I'd give the two dollars. After church a couple invited us over to their house for goodies. While we were there, the husband took me aside. 'I don't know why I should do this,' he told me, 'but I really feel that I should give you two dollars,' That's a fast return!"

If you're giving only 10 percent, or if you're not giving before you spend, or if you're not expecting a return from your giving, you may not be receiving any blessing from your giving either. But that's easy to turn around. Let me tell you about four ways to receive blessing through giving.

GET BLESSED BY GIVING GENEROUSLY.

I heard recently about the comment of a Christian man who had observed the lifestyle of some full-time Christian workers.

"I really see how they have to trust God an awful lot," he observed. "They get no salary from the organization they work for, and they're supported only by the gifts of people, so their income always varies. If they have a need, and not enough money, they really have to live by faith. But I wonder about guys like me. I earn a set income, and have it all budgeted out to meet our needs. How do people like me learn to live by faith?"

There are several answers to his question, but the easiest is simply to begin to give more. If you're giving to God now, and still have everything all planned to fit into your budget, then maybe you should start giving by faith. When you hear about a couple you know who have four kids under five years of age, and they don't have money, buy them a dishwasher. It's as you start responding to the needs of those around you by faith, trusting God to care for your needs in return, that you open the door for God to begin to really bless you.

A couple decided to take $500 out of their savings account to help meet needs of others they'd heard about. When the wife went to the savings and loan company to get the money, she felt the Spirit was prompting her to take out an extra $100 to make it $600 to give, and that night they sent the money off. Two days later their income tax man called to ask if they would read him some figures from their records of two years back, saying he might have made a mistake. After going over the figures he called back with the news that he *had* made a mistake. He refiled for them, and they got back $600 they had overpaid.

GET BLESSED
BY GIVING AWAY THINGS YOU NEED.

Remember the situation when Jesus miraculously fed the five thousand? Their need was for food, and the provision began when the little boy gave away his lunch. That boy's bread and fish became more bread and fish— not pepperoni pizza. I asked a group once, "What if that boy's lunch had been Kentucky Fried Chicken? What would the crowd have eaten that day?" The answer came back unanimously: "*Buckets* of Kentucky Fried Chicken!" So if you find yourself going twenty-six hours a day and you need more time, look for someone who's going twenty-eight, give them a couple of hours of your time, and expect God to bless you in return with still more time.

GET BLESSED BY "GIVING"
WHAT SOMEONE HAS TAKEN FROM YOU.

Jesus said, "If any one would sue you and take your coat, let him have your cloak as well" (Matthew 5:40). Is that what you'd tell a friend who was being taken to court? Ninety-five percent of the population today would say, "Countersue! You've got your rights!"

God's advice is the opposite. He sees all those situations in which your "rights" are being violated as opportunities for him to bless you. So when you're imposed upon or taken advantage of, don't just take it lying down, but don't fight back, either. *Give* that money or that time or that business deal to God as a gift, just as if you'd decided all on your own to give it. Then expect him to bless you. He will.

A few years ago, when I was selling real estate, a friend I had been working with called and asked if I would write up a contract on a house. After getting the contract and loan application approved, I received a letter from another realtor saying that the commission on that sale should be his. I showed the letter to my broker, and he disagreed, so he told me to write the realtor back, explaining how the house had sold, which I did.

By return mail, the realtor told me he was going to take me to court for the commission. He had had a minor involvement with this couple and with the house, so he thought this merited the commission. I considered fighting for it, but I decided I wouldn't—by faith. I called him and told him that if he felt he deserved all the commission, it was his, and that I would be happy with his decision.

He decided to keep $640 of the commission and give me $139. So I told God I wanted to up my giving $640 that month.

Shortly after that, Bill Christenson, a friend who was a realtor in another city, called and said he had clients here in Colorado Springs who needed to sell their house. He asked if I would go down and talk to them about listing it, and two and a half hours later, it sold for full price. My commission was $840.

You won't lose by giving to God what someone takes from you. Just expect God to multiply it back to you. "Give and it shall be given to you," said Jesus, "good measure, pressed down, shaken together, running over" (Luke 6:38).

GET BLESSED BY EXPECTING A RETURN.
Some people give but don't receive in return because they don't *expect* any. Have you ever said, "I give even

if God never gives back to me, because I just love to give?"
That's noble, but it's not what God meant when he
said, "Open your mouth wide, and I will fill it" (Psalm
81:10). If you don't open up, expecting to receive,
there just won't be any place for God to put his blessing.
As Dr. Theodore Epp of Back to the Bible Broadcast
has said, "God gives to everyone, but he will give more if
we are expecting it."

Don't be confused by expecting to receive from those
to whom you gave. *God* is the One who gives back,
and he usually uses *other* people or circumstances to
reward you. That's why you need to keep an eye open
for returns from your giving. If you don't, you might
not recognize them when they come.

Giving: it's a great potential for blessing to you—if
you're expecting God to give back to you as he promised
he would.

SEVEN
PATIENCE: FAITH'S RIGHT ARM

Be ... imitators of those who through faith and patience inherit the promises (Hebrews 6:12).

Sometimes the stories are really exciting, like the man in New Mexico who told how he'd needed a car. He told God he'd take whatever God chose, but the car he'd *really* like would be:
—2 years old
—metallic brown with a white racing stripe
—compact with good gas mileage
—carpeted, with a white interior and a radio
—three-speed on the floor without bucket seats (although he'd never seen a three-speed on the floor with anything *but* bucket seats)
—air conditioned
—white vinyl topped
—priced below $2,500.
The next day he went shopping, and the first place he went, there stood the car he'd described to God the day before, perfect to the last detail. And it had only 7,000 miles on it.
Other times the stories are more like the young couple

who wrote me sharing the list of five things they'd asked God for. God had done all five, but they observed, "Our timing was off. We desired our faith goals to be answered in three months but it took six." So they wound up with a three-month wait to see God work.

But three months is a drop in the bucket compared to the wait God asks of some of his children.

It was twenty-five years from the time God promised Abraham that he would be the father of a great nation to the actual birth of his son Isaac. Joseph waited from his boyhood to probably nearly age forty for the fulfillment of the dream the Lord had given him that his brothers would bow down to him with respect. Noah waited most of his adult life for the promised flood.

God promises only that he will do what you ask; he doesn't say when.

It's like what God told Habakkuk. "But these things I plan won't happen right away. Slowly, steadily, surely, the time approaches when the vision will be fulfilled. If it seems slow, do not despair, for these things will surely come to pass. Just be patient! They will not be overdue a single day!" (Habakkuk 2:3, TLB).

But it's in this time-lag that you can easily lose heart. You've begun by faith, trusting God to meet this need or that; you've prayed; you've chosen not to look to any other resource. And then: nothing. It's probably because this waiting period is such a common experience that Hebrews 6:12 says, "Be imitators of those who through faith *and patience* inherit the promises." Faith is half the story of seeing God work. Patience is the other half.

If God does not fulfill every one of your requests right now, it's not because he is toying with you, or because he is cruel, or because he is powerless, or because he's waiting for someone's permission. Isaiah 30:18 says, "Therefore the Lord waits *to be gracious to you*." God

often waits because your dreams are not big enough,
or because you aren't yet big enough for your dreams.

MAYBE YOUR DREAMS AREN'T BIG ENOUGH.

A few years ago Patti and I started looking for a different
house. We wanted a bigger one and one in the same
area so the kids wouldn't have to change schools. After
several months of searching, a house came on the
market that was the size we were after and in our price
range, so we called the realtor and put in a bid on it.

But the next day, we found out that another Christian
had also made an offer on the house, and his offer
exactly matched ours. Even though this was the first
house we'd seen in months that even came close to what
we wanted, we felt an inward caution. We decided
we should withdraw our bid for the sake of the other
bidder, and let God give us the house if he wanted
to. But the other bid was accepted and we were back to
looking and waiting.

Within two months another house came up for sale.
This one was ten years newer; it had a double garage
instead of a single; it was perched on the edge of a
20-acre park; and we got it for $1,000 less than the house
we'd wanted so badly. God asked us to wait because
our dream just wasn't big enough.

Joseph's dream was that his family would bow down to
him, but God saw that scene as only a small part
of his dream for Joseph. When God fulfilled the dream,
many years later, not only Joseph's family but all
of Egypt was bowing to him.

I was taking part in a service in South Africa honoring
retiring missionaries of a certain board when I met
a woman whose dreams had needed expanding, and time
was the instrument God used. When she had first come
to the field, that woman wanted to work in a particular

compound because she felt she'd be most effective there. She prayed about it and argued with the board about it, but their decision was to send her to another field. She went, but she was disappointed about their decision and about her unanswered prayer.

As the years went on in her new field, a need arose for holiday Bible schools to reach children for Christ, and she began developing materials for them. No one knew that she had talent for such work, but the materials she developed were so good that they became widely used throughout the area in children's ministries.

At that retirement ceremony she acknowledged to her co-workers how the Lord had arranged for her a much bigger impact than she'd imagined, and he had accomplished it by having her wait for the answers to her prayers. She had ministered to the field she'd prayed for, through the materials she had written, and to many other fields besides. Her dreams just needed expanding, and it took a time-lag that required some patient waiting.

A couple I met in Oregon were going into commercial fishing and needed a boat, so they put together the opportunities and their resources, and decided they could afford a forty-foot or fifty-foot one.

The first boat they found looked perfect, and both of them thought, "This is it!" But the boat was sold to someone else. When they found the second boat, they both said, "*This* boat would really satisfy us; it has everything we'd ever need!" But that boat, too, was sold to someone else.

Then word came of some possibilities in Mobile, Alabama, so they took off to investigate three boats there. Surely with *three* to choose from... But all three turned out to be junkers.

It looked as if the dream was not working out, but that was just because it wasn't big enough yet.

While they were in Mobile they met a boat builder from

Louisiana who suggested he could build them what they wanted and have it ready in six months, but there was one problem. The boat he was talking about was a seventy-five footer—nearly twice as big as they'd originally considered or dreamed they could afford.

"But we have a God who rewards," the wife said. "The finances were arranged and we're now the happy owners of a beautiful seventy-five-foot boat that is three or four times the value of what we would have considered originally."

Sometimes God has to wait to make your dreams as big as his are.

MAYBE YOU AREN'T BIG ENOUGH FOR YOUR DREAMS.

If the Lord had answered Abraham's prayers for a son during the first year after he'd left Haran for the Promised Land, it might not have been the best for Abraham. I wonder if Abraham would yet have been a man of enough character and depth and trust in God to meet the tests that were ahead—tests like God's command to offer Isaac as a sacrifice to him. Would Abraham have been obedient?

But those twenty-five years of waiting for a son gave Abraham a chance to grow into a man big enough to measure up to the dream of being the one through whom all the families of the earth would be blessed. He was a big enough man to be the father of one child when he left Haran, but only after twenty-five years of growing and testing was he ready to be the father of faith, the father of all who trust Jesus Christ. God delayed his promise to Abraham in order to give Abraham time to become big enough for his dreams.

Patience is not a cowardly, feeble spirit. It's not being too weak to stand up for your rights. Patience is the aggressive power which enables a man to persevere steadfastly through the most adverse circumstances.

Such faith is what the martyrs had when they died singing. That's why Paul prayed, "May you be strengthened with all power, according to his glorious might, for all endurance and patience with joy" (Colossians 1:11).

HOW TO HAVE PATIENCE WHEN GOD SAYS, "WAIT."

You are surrounded by the "now" generation, so having to wait for anything is just not part of the American scene. How do you wait on God with the kind of patience that keeps you trusting and rejoicing?

A lot of your success will come from realizing that in God's perspective, problems are just incomplete blessings, and patience allows blessings to come from those problems.

James 1:2-7 talks about problems, and how to have patience through them. I like the simple little three-step plan it gives to let you know what to do to keep trusting through the problems.

1. *Be glad about your troubles because you see a long-range plan.* "Dear brothers, is your life full of difficulties and temptations? Then be happy, for when the way is rough, your patience has a chance to grow. So let it grow, and don't try to squirm out of your problems. For when your patience is finally in full bloom, then you will be ready for anything, strong in character, full and complete" (James 1:2-4, TLB).

Don't rejoice in hard times because you have masochistic tendencies, or because you like to punish yourself. Rejoice because you see the long-range picture of who God is and that he will bring good to you from the trouble. The testing of your faith produces steadfastness which in the end will make you perfect and complete, lacking in nothing. You can't be glad to suffer, but you can be glad about becoming mature and complete.

You can be like the businessman here in Colorado Springs who suffered his first really big financial setback and got so mad that he kicked a door and broke his foot. That is *not* being mature and complete.

In contrast, a lady told me that they had a fire in their basement, and as she stood in the yard waiting for the fire truck to come, she thought to herself, "I may just as well go ahead and thank God for this fire now, because he's sure to bring good to us out of it, and I'll save myself a lot of time." And that's just what happened.

So when your seventh-grader fails math, or your water heater gives out, or your wife gets sick, meet it with joy and thanks to God. You're not thankful for the bad times but for the maturing you're going to get out of it.

It's interesting that Saul, Israel's first king, didn't last long as God's man. Yet his successor, David, took the nation to great power and became a man after God's heart in the midst of similar circumstances. The two had much in common in their natural abilities, but with Saul, things always came easily. He was tall and good-looking, a sort of golden-boy, who apparently never went through much difficulty before he was chosen to be king—and he crumpled.

But David's way was not so smooth. He went through years of hiding in the wilderness and fleeing from Saul before he got the throne, and because he did endure hardness he was ready to lead the nation in the knowledge of God. It was those troubles that God used to produce the maturity that made David's life full and successful in the long run.

Meet troubles with thanksgiving—because you know the author of the long-range plan.

2. *Ask for wisdom.* "If you want to know what God wants you to do, ask him, and he will gladly tell you, for he is always ready to give a bountiful supply of wisdom to all who ask him; he will not resent it" (James 1:5, TLB).

When troubles come, it's often not clear just what

to do. But that's the time to claim God's promise to give
you wisdom generously, because that promise was
written expressly to those who are going through rough
times.

A lady told about her refrigerator breaking down when
she wasn't financially set to get another one. No
refrigerator and no cash, and the episode took place in the
heat of the summer. The first solution that popped
into her head was to go ahead and get one—and charge it.

But the Lord used a friend to give her his wisdom
in meeting the trial, and the friend encouraged her to see
what God would do instead of trusting her credit. So
she decided to give God a month.

A few days later her sister called, asking if she'd like a
new refrigerator *free*. "A couple of months ago we
bought a refrigerator," the sister explained, "and the
other day at a new store grand opening, we won another
one. We sure don't need two."

Ask God how to meet the problem, and his wisdom will
work things out for your best.

3. *Don't doubt.* "He who doubts," the Bible says, "is like
a wave of the sea that is driven and tossed by the
wind. For that person must not suppose that a
double-minded man, unstable in all his ways, will receive
anything from the Lord" (James 1:6-8).

Just because you have a need, ask God's help, and
nothing happens right that second, don't conclude that
God isn't going to work.

A girl made a decision in college to give her life to Jesus
Christ and had begun growing spiritually. Then she
got sick and got so far behind in her school work that she
had to drop out of school. She looked at the circumstances
and concluded that God had let her down. Her sister
told me that she has never recovered in her spiritual life.

If you decide to doubt what God has said and what
he can do, you are the one who loses. That girl lost the

peace and joy of trusting Christ, and she lost a lifetime of adventure following his perfect plan for her.

God's timetable is often different from yours, and it's always better. So make patience the right arm of your faith, and all that God has promised you will be yours.

EIGHT
PROMISES, PROMISES

He staggered not at the promise of God through unbelief;
but was strong in faith, giving glory to God;
... being fully persuaded that what he had promised,
he was able also to perform (Romans 4:20, 21, KJV).

Have you ever wondered what life would be like if you
took all the TV commercials at their word? The right
toothpaste could turn even Cinderella's ugly step-sister
into a sex goddess. Detergents would put giants in
your washing machine. You'd believe your crackers were
made by little elves. Promises, promises. None of
them true.

When a man with Merrill Lynch called a client to see if
she'd received some information he'd mailed her a few
days before, he lamented, "I don't have a lot of faith in the
postal system anymore. As I get older, I get more
skeptical—or maybe just more realistic!"

At one time a man's word was usually enough. A
handshake could close a business deal involving great
sums of money. But those days are gone, except with God.

With God it has been, and is, and always will be
true that when he says it, it will happen. "God is not man,

that he should lie," says Numbers 23:19, "or a son
of man, that he should repent. Has he said, and will he
not do it? Or has he spoken, and will he not fulfill it?"

Faith is believing what God has said, not how you feel,
not what your friends say, not how the circumstances
look, not what seems logical to you, not what the
newspaper reports, not what experience has taught you.
Living by faith means believing what God has said.
When God promises, it's as good as done.

KNOW GOD'S PROMISES.
Satan started his attack on mankind by coming to Eve
with: "Hath God said...?" With that question Satan
confused Eve about the word of God. And he is still at it.

A church-funded medical center I just read about
had been doing a thriving business in sex-change
operations. When the hospital board decided that in light
of Scripture an institution representing Jesus Christ
should not be doing such things, the doctors'
representative came before them and pled, "When Christ
was on earth, he was kind to everyone. So if he were
here today, I'm sure he'd help anyone who's unhappy.
Can we expect the fine Christian doctors performing
these operations to do any less than what Christ
would do?"

Jesus once rebuked the Pharisees, saying, "You are
wrong, because you know neither the Scriptures nor
the power of God" (Matthew 22:29). He'd probably make
the same accusation today.

Not long ago, I met a discouraged, disillusioned
pastor's wife at a Christian conference, who confided to
me that most of her seventy years had been a
roller-coaster spiritual existence. "I come to these
conferences every year," she complained, "and they
really put me on a spiritual high, but then I go home and
the other fifty-one weeks of the year I'm at a low.

It's been a miserable way to live." I'm sure she was not exaggerating.

Not long afterwards, I met another elderly Christian couple who told me nearly the same story. Their highs came a little more frequently because they went to a church with a terrific Bible teacher, and that one hour each Sunday was a pepper-upper; but their general life-graph looked like a kid's drawing of ocean waves.

That lasted until they joined a small group Bible study where they learned how to dig into the Scriptures for themselves and apply those truths to their own lives. Then both John and his wife started chewing up the Word daily, and began experiencing the stability and growth they'd hoped for for years.

Paul would have given both the pastor's wife and that couple the same advice if he'd heard their troubles. "I commend you to God and *to the word of his grace*, which is able to build you up" (Acts 20:32). He would not have commended them to just some sweet fellowship or to the Wednesday night prayer meeting. He left them in the hands of *the Word of God*, because knowing the Word would give them access to the power they needed for a fruitful, growing life.

LET GOD'S PROMISES
DIRECT YOU TO THE PROMISOR.

When the angel came to Sarah to tell her she would become the mother of a child at age ninety, Sarah burst out laughing at such a ridiculous idea. But after that initial reaction she chose to believe the promise anyway. Hebrews 11:11 says, "She considered *him* faithful who had promised." The promise did sound crazy, but she knew God wasn't, so she believed it would happen just as he had said.

You can come to know the Promisor by investigating what he has and has not said he will do. God has never promised to keep all trouble away from you, but he *has* promised to provide all you need to meet those troubles with joy, and to cause all the troubles to work together for your good. He has never promised that every step you take in obedience to his will would result in your instant popularity, but he *has* promised that whatever you lose in man's esteem he'll make up to you himself. "For my father and my mother have forsaken me, but the Lord will take me up" (Psalm 27:10).

Getting to know God's promises is not hard. Don't be scared off by the fact that people seem to come up with so many conflicting ideas from the Bible. It's true that you can "prove" anything with Scripture, but it depends on whether your intent is to conform God to your way of life, or to conform your way of life to God's. If you're out to be God's person, and if you want to know what he wants and how he can help, then you'll find God's promises easy to grasp and follow. Four simple guidelines will help you as you read the Bible.

1. *Ask the Spirit's help.* To be understood, and to be a foundation for your faith, the promises of God must be read with the same Spirit that originally inspired them. Such help is the Holy Spirit's job description. "When the Spirit of truth comes, he will guide you into all the truth" (John 16:13). You may as well let him do his job. Just ask him, as you begin to read the Bible, to show you God's thinking, and what God wants you to know from what you're reading. Then listen.

2. *Be objective, not emotional.* A Christian woman was counseling with her brother about his decision to leave his wife and family to marry another woman. She opened *The Living Bible* to Malachi 2:15-16 and read to him, "You were united to your wife by the Lord. In God's wise plan, when you married, the two of you became one person in his sight. And what does he want?

Godly children from your union. Therefore guard
your passions! Keep faith with the wife of your youth.
For the Lord, the God of Israel, says he hates
divorce and cruel men. Therefore control your passions—
let there be no divorcing of your wives."

The man sat there a moment in silence and then said,
"Does this mean you won't come to the wedding?"

He was so emotionally involved in the situation, so set
on his own way, that he couldn't even hear what the
Bible said.

I met a man a couple of years ago who was in love with
a girl who lived several thousand miles away. He
didn't see her often, but he was continually "finding"
verses that he took to mean God intended for them
to marry. Imagine the blow when he came back from
overseas, and found she'd married someone else.
Emotions can sometimes cause you to find things in the
Word of God that really aren't there.

So check yourself. Ask, "If somebody else read this
passage I just did, what would *he* say it was saying?"

3. *Look at the context to help find the meaning.* A friend
of mine told me that when he started a campus Christian
work in Pennsylvania, he and another man walked
around the campus and claimed God's promise in Joshua
1:3: "Every place that the sole of your foot will
tread upon, I have given to you, as I promised to Moses."

If you read the story in Joshua 1, this promise was
one to Joshua, and it concerned the geography of Canaan,
not some place in Pennsylvania. But the principle
of the verse is that God was leading Joshua to take the
land for his glory, and that God would go before
him and give it to him. My friend was out to reach
students for Christ on that campus in obedience to God,
and he was trusting God to do the work. The fact
of God's help for such a situation is confirmed many other

places in Scripture, so he could feel confident in
claiming the lives of Satan's people on that campus for
God—and using Joshua 1:3 to do it.

4. *Relate the promises to your own life.* It's wonderful
to know that God has promised to supply all your
needs, but what specific need do you have today for God
to meet? He's promised direction. What decision are
you facing, for which you can claim his guidance?

BELIEVE THE PROMISES.
Myron Rush was a student at Central Missouri State
University in Warrensburg when a math instructor
there led him to Jesus Christ. Myron started to grow
spiritually and he thought he believed the Bible,
but not until a need arose did he discover the difference
between knowing and believing.
    Myron had been preaching in a little church that paid
him $45 a week to help support his wife and two
children while he went to school. But after he met Christ,
his preaching changed and the church fired him.
    "Believe me," he told me, "I was low and I didn't know
which way to turn. But Carl, who had led me to Christ,
came by and showed me in Matthew 6:33 that God
has promised to take care of us."
    After Carl had read the verse to Myron, he asked,
"Do you believe that?"
    "Of course I believe that," Myron responded, surprised.
    "You don't either," Carl countered.
    "Yes, I do," Myron insisted.
    "I know you don't believe it," Carl said, "because if
you did, you'd have no concern about how you're going
to provide for school or for your family without that
church job."
    Knowing is the beginning, but believing God's promises

requires grabbing them and saying, "That's for *me*."
David took this attitude in 2 Samuel 17. After David
had taken the kingship of Israel, God gave him a whole
chapterful of promises. David knew what God was
promising, but in verse 25 he showed that he took those
promises seriously. He said, "And now, O Lord God,
confirm forever the word which thou hast spoken
concerning thy servant and concerning his house, and do
as thou hast spoken." God stopped speaking to David,
and David started speaking to God. Can't you see
David almost giving God an order? He looks God squarely
in the eye and tells God to commit himself. After
God spoke, David *believed* what God had said.

CLAIM THE PROMISES.
Claiming God's promises means acting as if they're true
for you.
    When God told Noah there was going to be a flood,
Noah acted as if it was true, and started building an ark.
When God told Moses there would be a way for the
people of Israel through the Red Sea, Moses acted as if
it was true, and stepped into the water.
    There are two ways to "act as if" a promise of God is
true for you.

1. *You can claim the promise by fulfilling its conditions.*
Mary Irwin tells about taking hold of God's promise
for her garden when grasshoppers were eating the
vegetables alive. Mary didn't want to use a commercial
insecticide on her organic garden, so she went to
the Bible and checked among the 3,753 promises there
for one about grasshoppers, and she found one. "I will
rebuke the devourer for you," Malachi 3:11 says,
"so that it will not destroy the fruits of your soil; and
your vine in the field shall not fail to bear, says the

Lord of hosts." In this instance the *if*—condition attached
to the promise—is one verse ahead. It says to bring
the tithes into the store house, to give God his due.

So Mary claimed the promise by checking to be sure she
and her husband had fulfilled the condition of giving
God his share from what he'd already provided for them.
Her husband confirmed that they had, so she told
God he was committed now to take care of those
grasshoppers.

"It didn't happen overnight," Mary related. "I feel
perhaps God was testing me for a while to either trust him
or trust commercial spray to take care of the
grasshoppers. Many times during the next few days I
was tempted to take matters into my own hands,
but I was always reminded that God's arm was not short
concerning me."

God did what that Malachi verse promised. The tall
grass around their garden was dry and had to be burned
off, and in the burning, 99 percent of the grasshoppers
were destroyed.

You can claim God's promises, acting as if they're
true, by fulfilling the conditions that accompany
the promises. Second Corinthians 9 is full of promises
of God's abundant supply and blessing, but 9:7 says that
to qualify for those promises you need to be a cheerful
giver. Romans 8:28 promises that everything will
work for your very best—if you fulfill the condition of
being God's and responding to him.

Act as if God's promises are true by fulfilling their
conditions.

2. *You can claim God's promises by taking the next
obvious step.* When I was just out of college I took a job
which involved supervising the work of eight other
men. Before the first Monday morning, I carefully came
up with a work plan, but by five o'clock that night, we

had done everything I'd planned for the whole week!

That night, I woke up at about 3:00 A.M., terrified. "What on earth am I going to do with those eight guys tomorrow?" I thought. "I'm going to get out there and really look foolish." Then I remembered a verse I had memorized sometime before. "Fear not; for I am with you, be not dismayed, for I am your God; I will strengthen you, I will help you, I will uphold you with my victorious right hand" (Isaiah 41:10). I decided that if that was true, I might as well act as if it was, and go back to sleep.

The next day went great, but the following night at about 3:00 A.M. I again woke up with the same fear of "what'll we do tomorrow?" Again God gave me his promise. Again I decided that if it was true, I'd better get some sleep. Sure enough, the next day went great, too. And the next. Pretty soon I wasn't waking up anymore, because I had claimed God's promise, and he had proved himself.

If you know and believe God's promise in Matthew 28:18 that all authority on heaven and earth belongs to Christ, then you can act as if it's true by doing what verse 19 says: going and making disciples of all nations. If you believe God has promised you a trip to Europe, you'll keep your passport up to date. Claiming God's promises happens when you act as if they are true.

A soldier I met several years ago in Viet Nam told of his chance to act on God's promise. He and his company had been fighting hard for days, and they were worn out. One night they'd stopped to rest, totally exhausted. But just as they dropped to the ground, the enemy began to fire mortars at them over a hill.

"I can't sleep here," he thought immediately. "With those mortars firing, I'll be killed." But then God's promise of his protection came to mind. And the soldier decided that if the promise was true, then what he needed was rest, and rest was what he'd do. So he lay down on the ground and got a full night's sleep while the shells exploded around him. God faithfully protected his life, just as he'd promised.

Living by faith means living and acting in light of what God has said he will do. You have to know what he's said, believe it, and then claim it as your own.

NINE
HOW TO PLAN BY FAITH

*Truly, truly, I say to you, he who believes in me will also
do the works that I do; and greater works than these
will he do ...* (John 14:12).

"The man without a plan is always at the mercy of the
man with a plan." That's the motto of a person I know, and
it's not a bad one. If you've read the book of Proverbs
you're aware that God is certainly in favor of planning.
"We should make plans," Proverbs 16:9 directs, "counting
on God to direct us."

God himself is a planner. He has a well-laid and orderly
plan for the world from Day One until its end; and
he has plans for you, according to Jeremiah 29:11. God
decided on his plan for the world long before it was
ever created, and he did the same with his plans for you.
In Psalm 139 David says to God, "You saw me before
I was born and scheduled each day of my life before I
began to breathe. Every day was recorded in your
Book!" (Psalm 139:16, TLB). How's that for an example
of detailed planning—and planning ahead!

Probably one reason why you might be seeing so little
happening in your life is that you're aiming at

nothing, and hitting it. Do you know where you're going? Do you see clearly where you want to head in your family life, in your business, in your outreach to others? What are your plans?

I sat in a Christian conference once where the subject was how to plan, and the topic was all sewn up. We took pencil and paper and wrote O-A-T-S as the vertical word of an acrostic. For the O we each wrote out objectives. The A stood for activities we'd do to fulfill our objectives. Then for the T we put down our timetable for accomplishment, and for the S we indicated the systematic checkup we'd use to make sure it was all done.

A little system like OATS may make you a better businessman, because some book on management is probably where OATS came from. But using it won't necessarily make you a person of faith. God never promises to pour out his blessings on OATS or on good managers, but only on people who exercise faith.

That's why God warns of hard times ahead for people who "ask advice from everyone but me, and decide to do what I don't want you to do" (Isaiah 30:1, TLB). In this case the Israelites' objective (to be saved from the invaders) made sense, and their activities (to go to Egypt for help) looked logical in light of that objective, but the plan was doomed to failure because it lacked one vital ingredient: *dependence on God's resources*. The plan was not a plan of faith because it did not need God's intervention to make it work.

I got an exciting letter not long ago from a woman who had read my first book and discovered this difference between making her own plans, and planning in faith.

I was saved four years ago, and since I had done quite a bit of writing before, I naturally thought, "Oh, boy, I'll write for the Lord." However, it didn't work out that way. Everything I wrote went into the circular file.

*It took four years' worth of prayer (mine and others') and
agonizing (mine alone) to realize why I could no longer
write.*

*Since I could always squeeze a nickel in my pocket
until the Indian came out riding the buffalo, the idea of
giving to God really appealed to me. I gave him my
tongue, which has usually been sharper than a—well,
I guess you get the picture. The success of my column
had depended on my subtle rabbit punches to the
other guy's ego.*

*Russ, I know you won't be surprised at all to learn
what happened. The next three magazines I read (one
Christian, two secular) had articles about cleaning up
our language. I turned on the TV, and the commentary
was concerned with foul language in books. When I
went to work, my boss got into the act.*

*"Look, if you want to use a word, use it; but stop
making those cute approximations," he told me. I have
never before been so conscious of language, the writer's
primary tool.*

*After much underlining and many notes in the
margins, and after reading your book a second time, I
wrote this prayer at the end of chapter one: My
prayer is that you will use my writing ability to help
others.*

*Oh-oh. Something was wrong. I had very graciously
conceded that the Lord worked through you, but with me
it was my ability that was going to change the world.
This was the way I had been praying for four years.
No wonder God hadn't honored a prayer like that.
Without God I have nothing; without God I am nothing.*

*How glad I am that Jesus is at the Throne interceding
for us, for I'm sure what poured out would have made no
sense otherwise. In among the gulps, tears, and
confessions, I told God that if he did intend to use me in
the writing field, he'd just have to get me a typewriter.
No self-respecting editor would ever look at a manuscript*

that came from my old worn-out machine. This happened in the morning.

That afternoon a lady laid a sealed envelope on my kitchen table. It would take another letter to explain why she thought she was in debt to me, but it was what she said that was important. "I want you to take this money and put it toward a new typewriter." Well, the showers of tears that morning were nothing compared with the torrents that rushed forth. I kept saying, "It works—it really works!" I praised the Lord and thanked him for understanding and answering my prayer.

Since the money was only half of what I needed, I should have known God wasn't through. When I got to work that night (I teach adult education), the director insisted on reimbursing me for something I had purchased on my own. This brought my typewriter fund close to the two-thirds mark, so I decided to make up the difference.

The business machine agency I dealt with was fifty miles away, and I don't drive, so the next problem was how to get there. By now I didn't think of it as a problem, though, and I just sat back and waited on the Lord.

Another day passed, and my husband decided to take the day off to go deer hunting. But as he pushed back from the breakfast table, there stood a deer outside the window. After he had shot it, got it inspected, and hung it in the barn, there was plenty of time to take me to get the typewriter.

Perhaps letter writing will be my ministry, and I may never see another by-line, but I know the Lord will use his typewriter in his own way.

P.S. I've just received another gift specifically given for the typewriter. You not only can't outdo the Lord, you can't even match him!

One of Donna's plans, to become a Christian writer, wound up with four years' worth of writing that led nowhere. But her second plan, to get a typewriter worked. The difference? The plan for the typewriter was a plan *by faith* that God wanted to work on her behalf.

MAKE GOD-SIZED PLANS.

When my friend Stan began trying to rent out a garage he owned, he put an ad in the paper and got no response to it at all. And he said to me, "I'll bet that garage isn't renting because the price is too low. I think I'll raise what I'm asking and try it again."

That's what you call a big thinker. The other 99.9 percent of the population would have thought, "It's not renting because I'm asking *too much*—I need to lower the price." But Stan had probably heard about the perfume manufacturers who discovered that most of their perfumes sold better at higher prices than at lower ones. If women didn't have to pay much for the fragrance, they figured it was "cheap" perfume and wanted no part of it.

Somebody in Christian circles is propagating the idea that small is better than big. If you get through the month without going in debt, and get through your marriage without getting a divorce, and get through your work life without being fired, that's enough to ask. And we sing enthusiastically, "Brighten the corner where you are," when God's goals are more like "Transform the world where you are."

An assistant minister in Minneapolis and his church's young people were studying Matthew 16:18, where Jesus says that he will build his church, and the gates of hell will not prevail against it. According to Jesus' picture, the place with big walls around it is hell, and the church is marching aggressively against hell to knock down those gates. Those young people couldn't see that picture. Each time they went over the passage, they came to the same conclusion: the church was the place surrounded by a big wall and huge gates to keep out evil, and the forces of hell were storming those walls, trying to break them down and get inside. They'd become so accustomed to thinking defensively about the church's mission in the world that God's challenge to claim people and governments and continents for him could not penetrate. Planning by faith means having big plans, God-sized plans.

The plans and goals God gave to people have two consistent elements: a *worldwide* influence, and a *lasting* impact. That's much more than brightening the corner where you are.

Look at the goal he gave to Adam and Eve. "Be fruitful and multiply and fill the earth and subdue it" (Genesis 1:28). He could have told them to be fruitful and raise a couple of good kids, but he didn't. His plan for them was to fill the whole earth with people who loved him.

Or Abraham. God came to him and told him, "Go from your country and your kindred and your father's house to the land that I will show you. And I will make of you a great nation, and I will bless you, and make your name great so that you will be a blessing ... and by you all the families of the earth shall bless themselves" (Genesis 12:1-3).

There it is again. God didn't tell Abraham just to move, or just to have a son. His plan was that Abraham start a nation, and when he told Abraham that he'd be a blessing to all the families of the earth, that didn't just include the families of that generation. It meant families of all generations that would ever live on the earth. Now that's a *big* plan.

It's the same thinking pattern Jesus exhibited when he told his disciples, "But you shall receive power when the Holy Spirit has come upon you; and you shall be my witnesses in Jerusalem and in all Judea and Samaria and to the end of the earth" (Acts 1:8). If he'd just commanded them to testify to the people of Jerusalem, that probably would have been plenty to fill their thinking at that point. Just forty days earlier those people of Jerusalem were the very ones who put Jesus Christ to death, so to figure out a plan of how to witness to the Jerusalemites without all winding up dead would have probably been enough challenge to keep the disciples busy most of their lives.

Then Jesus told them to go on to the whole province of Judea, which was the "state" surrounding the city of Jerusalem.

Then he adds: "and to the end of the earth." Remember, this plan was given to men who lived long before the Boeing 747 and satellite communications. Most likely none of them had ever been out of the country of Palestine, and most of the traveling they'd ever done in their whole lives had been in the preceding three years when they walked the length and breadth of little Palestine with Jesus.

God-sized plans are big, big plans. If they're small enough for you to do them yourself, they aren't God-sized, and God won't get involved in them.

A husband and wife from Iowa attended a faith seminar I was teaching, and when I asked them to write down what they'd like to be doing in the next three months, both the husband and wife made identical lists. This was quite a "coincidence" in itself, since they were sitting on opposite sides of the room and hadn't conferred with each other. Both lists read: 1) Get out of debt. 2) Salvation for the wife's family.

The debt goal seemed more attainable than the second one, since the wife was from the East Coast and hadn't seen her family since she'd become a Christian. Also, her family was quite well spread out, so to get to all of them with the message would not be easy.

That goal of reaching her family was impossible enough, so God left it alone, apparently satisfied. But the other goal, getting out of debt, needed to be bigger before God would touch it, so he went to work to make it more impossible.

When the couple returned from the seminar to their home in Des Moines, Iowa, the "Here's Life, Des Moines" evangelistic campaign was in progress, and Norm felt a real urging to give to the campaign. But he had no money, and they were already in debt. The Spirit's urging persisted, however, and Norm could ignore it no longer. He did the only thing he could do: he went out and borrowed money to give to the "Here's Life" campaign.

Then the bottom fell out. Three days later Norm and Rose Marie got a call informing her that her father had died.

Norm recalls: "When we got that call, I thought the world was crashing in around me. It meant spending more money for plane tickets to the East Coast for the funeral. And I knew Rose's dad had veen living on Social Security disability payments for years, so I figured he'd surely have no money to pay for the funeral, and that would mean another expense. All this landed on top of our first debt, plus that second debt to give to 'Here's Life.' "

If there had been any human hope of bailing themselves out, that had long since grown dim. But that was the point at which God began to work.

When they flew to New York for the funeral, several family members commented on the tremendous change that had come about in both Norm's and Rose Marie's lives. Their new relationship with God was obvious, and it was apparently attractive, because the relatives asked Norm to get up during the funeral service and tell everyone about why his life had changed as much as it had. Norm did, and five people responded to Christ during the funeral. Another six did afterwards. Not bad for one Catholic funeral! In fact, not bad for a Baptist revival!

But God had not finished. Rose's dad had saved enough to take care of all the funeral expenses. And unknown to anyone else, he had also taken out insurance policies on his two youngest children (including Rose Marie) when they were very young. When the first policy was cashed, it came to the exact amount they had borrowed to give to "Here's Life." And when they cashed the other policy later, it was worth enough to get them completely out of debt.

Make plans, but be sure they are plans that are *big enough for you to need God's involvement.*

EXPECT GOD-SIZED RESOURCES TO FULFILL YOUR PLANS.

If you set for yourself or for your business a goal that you think you can handle, God will say, "Fine. Go ahead. It won't work out to my glory, but go ahead anyway."

You can't empty the ocean with a paper cup. You can't reach the moon in a Piper Cub, and you can't complete God-sized goals using human-sized resources. That's why you need to get your goals from God, determine not to limit yourself to your own resources, and let him do the doing in his own way.

A lady in a faith class I taught told me she'd come up with three goals as a result of the class. She'd asked God 1) for a new winter coat, 2) for the opportunity of leading a Jehovah's Witness to Christ, and 3) that a certain rotten school book would be banned from the school her child attended.

I asked her the next time I saw her how her three goals worked out.

"On the winter coat request," she answered, "I learned that next time I need to be more specific. When my mom came to visit us for Christmas, she got off the plane with a new mink coat for me draped over her arm. It's a winter coat all right, but next time I'm asking for a *practical* one. And I've led a Jehovah's Witness to Christ and am working on a second.

"And on that school book issue—I went to the school board meeting and got up and made a little speech against the book, but nobody listened. However, when the time came for a vote to be taken, one of the board members got confused about how the issue was worded, and mistakenly voted against the book. As a result, it was banned from the schools."

That lady allowed God to come through with his resources to accomplish his own goals.

A couple in our church in Colorado Springs took the faith class, and made it their faith-goal to see health for their daughter. The little girl had been born with severe physical handicaps, but had been seeing a specialist who had new treatment techniques, and the little girl had begun to develop. Then the doctor had died, and they had not been able to find another to help her. Her condition had regressed, and the parents were told not to expect their daughter to ever be much more than a vegetable. So they made a God-sized goal.

The mother wrote on her list: "Doctor to help my daughter as the other doctor did," and "Free medical care." (Her husband had just started his own business and their finances were very tight.) Then both drew back and waited. This was a God-sized job that would need some God-initiated resources.

God started working when Jane mistakenly left her purse at the beauty shop, and a friend dropped it off at her home.

"By the way, Jane," the woman said as she was leaving, "I know about the situation with your little girl needing special help. And I may have found a specialist in Denver who can work with her the way your other doctor did. Would you like to go to Denver with me this week, and we'll let him have a look at your child to see what he thinks?"

Jane agreed, and they saw the doctor.

The doctor's evaluation was positive. "I really think I can help your daughter," he told Jane, "and if you wouldn't be offended, I'd like to do it free." Jane wasn't in the least offended, and they began the treatments.

We heard from Dave and Jane not long ago, and they brought us up to date. "We've been keeping track, and it looks as if we've received at least $2,500 in medical treatments free," they reported. "And our little girl is doing so well. This fall she started school half-days, and we just got a call from her teacher telling us that she's making such good progress that they'd like to start having her stay full days."

If you're expecting God-inspired resources to accomplish your goals, quit thinking, "I wonder how this can ever work out." You'll never come up with the answer God has in his mind.

HOW TO KNOW
WHETHER YOUR PLANS ARE FAITH PLANS.

Here's a simple test by which to check your goals and plans to be sure they're by faith: *If it's by faith it will fail unless God intervenes.* That's what Paul was getting at when he said in 2 Corinthians 5:7: "For we walk by faith, not by sight." If you can see how it will all work out, then that's by sight, not by faith.

Putting down plans is for your good. "Where there is no vision, the people perish," says Proverbs 29:18, KJV. And visions call for God-sized plans. You'll get to know God as you let him help you plan, as you see him expand your thinking, and as he brings in incredible resources. It all starts with making *plans of faith.*

TEN
DEADLIER THAN DOUBT: BEING UNWILLING TO RECEIVE

Open your mouth wide, and I will fill it (Psalm 81:10).

Life is full of choices. If you're unconvinced of that, just decide you want to get a Chevy station wagon. Your decisions have just begun. Are you going to buy new or used? Which dealer are you going to go to? What options do you want? Colors? Interiors? How about a CB built in? Should you try your luck with one of those advertised in the want ads? How much less should you pay for a used one? And how used? What if the mileage isn't what the owner says it is? And what happens if something goes wrong?

Keep in mind that all these choices have cropped up *after* you've made the hardest choice of all—to actually buy a Chevy wagon. And that choice probably came after all kinds of hassles over "How badly do we really need it?" and "Would something else do as well?" Choices, choices. Man was barely created before he had to start making them.

And it's your basic capacity to make choices that will make all the difference in whether or not you live by faith. God will not force you to trust him or to experience all he has for you. You must choose to receive.

SOME WHO DID NOT RECEIVE.

Saul hadn't been king of Israel long when the Philistines
invaded Israel. He'd just ascended the throne a year
before, so he was really in need of something dramatic to
seal the kingdom as his own. That chance came with
the Philistines' invasion. Saul ordered up 3,000 special
troops, left 1,000 of them with his son Jonathan, and
set out for Gilgal. After Jonathan and his troops scored
a victory for Israel, the people got excited and came
to join Saul at Gilgal to go to war.

But what Israel met was a huge, swamping host of
Philistines, some 3,000 chariots and 6,000 horsemen, and
so many soldiers that "they were as thick as sand
along the seashore." Saul was prepared to sink the USS
Arizona, but what he faced was the Sixth Fleet.

Saul's army panicked and most of them went AWOL, so
Saul was left with 600 men against an enemy like
the sand of the sea. It was time for a choice and Saul made
the wrong one. The prophet Samuel had told Saul
specifically to wait for his arrival so that Samuel could
offer sacrifices to the Lord for Saul's victory. But
the Philistines looked ready for battle, Saul saw his army
slipping away, and Samuel didn't show in the seven
days he'd said he would, so Saul chose to go ahead and
offer the sacrifices himself.

It was a costly, costly choice. Samuel came on the
scene just as Saul was finishing the sacrifices. "You
fool!" Samuel exclaimed. "You have disobeyed the
commandment of the Lord your God. He was planning to
make you and your descendants kings of Israel forever,
but now your dynasty must end; for the Lord wants
a man who will obey him" (1 Samuel 13:13, 14, TLB). The
kingship didn't end that day, but it did end for Saul.

Saul died in dishonor and disgrace, and the eternal
throne of Israel went to David. God had been ready to
bestow on Saul a kingdom that would last forever,
but Saul chose not to receive it. David became the one

after God's own heart, not because God was kinder
to him, but because he chose to allow God to work in his
behalf. That's all God had asked of Saul, but Saul
refused and chose to try to take care of himself.

In a sermon which he calls "The Uniqueness of Jesus,"
Bill Bright of Campus Crusade for Christ tells of a
meeting at the Edgewater Hotel in Chicago in 1923.
Present were the president of the nation's largest
independent steel company, the president of the largest
utility company, the president of the largest gas
company, the greatest wheat speculator, the president of
the New York Stock Exchange, the president of the
International Bank of Settlements, and a member of the
President's cabinet. All these men had made life
choices, and had chosen to give themselves to money and
power. Here's what followed, twenty-five years later:

*Charles Schwaab, the steel company president, had died
in bankruptcy after living on borrowed capital for five
years.*

*Samuel Insull, the utility company president, had died
a fugitive from justice and penniless in a foreign land.*

*Howard Hopson, the gas company president, was
insane.*

*Arthur Cotton, the wheat speculator, had died abroad,
insolvent.*

*Richard Whitney, the Stock Exchange president, had
been released after being incarcerated in Sing Sing
Penitentiary.*

*Albert Fall, the member of the President's cabinet,
had been pardoned of a crime so he could die at home.*

*Jesse Livermore, known as the greatest bear on Wall
Street, had committed suicide.*

*Ivan Krueger, head of the greatest monopoly of his
time, had committed suicide.*

*Leon Frazer, the International Settlements Bank
president, had committed suicide.*

These men, like Saul, chose to live life their own way, and suffered the consequences.

The opportunities to choose whether or not you're going to let God care for you aren't usually too dramatic. It is what you do with the little choices of life that determines whether or not the big choices ever come to you. David got the chance to let God help him defeat Goliath because, quietly alone in the hills before, he'd chosen to receive God's help with a bear and a lion.

I wonder sometimes what happened to a young serviceman I met while I was in Okinawa. We were driving down the highway once when he brought up the problem of his radio.

"See, Russ," he told me, "I have time off during the day, so I'm around the barracks a lot, which wouldn't be a problem, except for this really nice radio I own. Other guys borrow it and turn on loud, wild music full blast, and I can't think, I can't read my Bible, I can't pray, I can't sleep. It's just ruining me."

I looked at him, surprised. "Whose radio is it again?"

"It's my radio," he responded.

"Have you ever thought of giving it away to some one who isn't in your barracks—or maybe even throwing it away? Do anything you need to to get it out of there!"

"But Russ," he came back, "it's a really nice radio."

He had to make a choice—a choice to get rid of the radio by faith and receive God's help and goodness to him in return, or to keep it. *No* radio is worth a trade-off like that!

He was like the woman who was at our house not long ago talking about a new job possibility opening up for her. The new job was a real step ahead, and it looked like an opportunity to which the Lord was really calling her. But she had to make a choice about her house. "I've thought of renting it," she told me, "but I've heard all these terrible stories about people wrecking it if you rent it out. And I *can't* sell it, because it's the only security I have on earth."

God was not asking that woman to choose between security and no security. He was asking her to choose between the security her little house could offer and the security the Eternal King of Glory could provide. He was asking her to be willing to receive something better than what she had. But she declined.

God won't force you to receive from him, but if you do choose to be a receiver, you can expect the resources of heaven to be available to you.

SOME WHO DID RECEIVE.

Chuck Axtell's job being in charge of one of the divisions of a trucking firm meant a great deal to him because he'd worked his way up from the bottom. But God asked him to choose between that job and something better— by faith.

It happened when Chuck's boss was going over the expense account records and found that Chuck hadn't submitted any bills for liquor to entertain customers. He called Chuck into his office to find out if there'd been a mistake on the receipts, but Chuck confirmed there'd been no mistake. Several months before, he'd given his life to Jesus Christ, and God had told him he should stop serving liquor to customers.

Chuck had decided instead to work harder at entertaining them other ways and after the football games and other activities he'd chosen, the customers had always responded warmly about the great time they'd had.

The boss listened to the story and then shook his head. "Chuck, you've done a good job here and we like you, but you've got to start serving liquor. According to company policy, we'll give you six months to change your mind on this."

Chuck had a choice to make: whether to look to his job as his resource, or to follow God and receive from his goodness.

Six months later, the boss called him in again. "Chuck," he said, "there's still no liquor charged to your expense account, so you can quit Wednesday or Friday." He took Friday.

Interestingly enough, the man Chuck had replaced in the company originally had been fired because he was an alcoholic, so it looks like you can't win either way—unless you're living by faith.

Chuck was out of work for a while, but during that time he received an inheritance that took care of his family's needs. And in the interim he spent several months with his family at a Christian training center, getting valuable help in Christian growth. Then the Lord opened up the chance to be the office manager for the upcoming Billy Graham Crusade in Omaha, Nebraska. And after the Crusade God placed him in a very successful job managing an office in Omaha. He wound up in a better position than the one he'd given up.

It's the same kind of experience that happened to a farmer in Iowa. Jerry knew how to grow corn, and had won the all-Iowa yield contest on land that had been in corn for ten consecutive years. Unless you're a farmer, that may not seem too earth-shattering, but take it from an ex-farmer: it's easier to grow good corn on land the first time around than the tenth. But then drought hit Iowa, and even prize-winning corngrowers can't raise corn without rain.

It was during the drought that Jerry told me God spoke to him from the Bible. "The passage I was reading," he explained, "talked about a drought like the one we were going through. And it said, 'The oil continued until the rains came' (1 Kings 17:16, TLB). Every previous time that we've had a rough time financially, I'd just tighten my belt and work through it on my own. I could trust myself and my own ability to make the money stretch, or I could be willing to receive from God, because God can supply even if we have no rain."

God won't make you receive if you don't want to, but if you're willing, he promises, "Put me to the test, says the Lord of hosts; see if I will not open the windows of heaven for you and pour down for you an overflowing blessing" (Malachi 3:10).

When Paul and Amy saw that the university had made a mistake, and the check they'd received was only half of what it should have been, they panicked. Paul was a student and their monthly pay wasn't covering expenses as it was.

"That check barely made the house payment," Amy recalled, "and we'd already borrowed from every place in town we could. Our Bankamericard was past due and we were over the credit limit. Four months earlier we had gotten a bill consolidation loan from the bank we still had to pay off, plus the home improvement loan we'd taken out. We owed Sears, Penney's, and Brandeis, and we'd also borrowed from friends. We'd already gotten a loan from the Credit Union at the university, and of course we had no savings. Every other loan place we could think of didn't give loans to students. We'd exhausted every possible source of additional income we could think of—except God."

They had tried to take care of themselves, and failed miserably. So Paul and Amy decided instead to let God take care of them.

They began by confessing the sin of handling their finances so poorly and then asked God to be their Supplier. But instead of just asking him to get them through the month, they made a list of *big* things they'd like God to do, like get them out of debt, get them a bigger house, and more. To show they were depending on God alone, they doubled their giving and cut up their credit cards.

God saw their hearts, and began to give in response. "We just sat back," Amy said, "and watched God pour in money from all sorts of places. Two months later,

our debt has decreased, we're living in a beautiful
new home, and our giving has quadrupled. God has
blessed us materially, but more important, he's given us
a new glimpse of his desire to be the Source of everything
we need."

Paul and Amy became receivers because they were
willing to let God give to them.

In 1966 I spent the summer in the Far East as part of
a Christian training program, and there I met Dr. Nathan
Banda, a Filipino physician. As I talked with him, I
recognized the seriousness of the choice Dr. Banda had
made to give his summer to spreading the gospel.

If you're a doctor in the Philippines, it's easy to get
work out in the villages, but that work pays little. And
since the livable incomes are all paid in Manila, that city
is glutted with doctors fighting for jobs. To get his
job in Manila, Dr. Banda had to work free for eight
months at the University of the East just to be hired.

About a year before we met, Dr. Banda had become a
Christian. When he heard about the program in which we
would be spending full time in witnessing and
Bible study, he felt that God wanted him to have such
an experience, so he went to his superiors at the
university and asked for a leave of absence.

"We're sorry," they replied. "There are far too many
other doctors standing in line for your job to give
you time off." But he chose to follow what God had told
him, and to let God do the worrying. He quit the job and
spent the summer reaching others for Christ.

A month and a half after I got back to America, I got a
call from a friend.

"I have sad news," he told me. "We've just received
word that Dr. Banda was in a motorcycle accident
in which he suffered a serious head injury. He's not
expected to live." He died shortly afterwards.

But imagine the glory that was waiting for him as he
left this life and came face to face with Jesus Christ's

greeting, "Well done, thou good and faithful servant. Enter into the joy of thy Lord!"

Dr. Banda didn't know that God was going to call him home to heaven at the end of that summer. But God knew. And God knew that the choice he asked Dr. Banda to make was not a foolish one. He was ready to pour blessing on Nathan Banda far beyond what he could have dreamed, and Dr. Banda chose to receive it.

In choosing God you never lose, because God has at his disposal all the resources you'll ever need. He has dreams for you that are so far beyond what you could create for yourself that you can't even imagine them.

Look to him, trust him, obey him. You'll find yourself living well beyond your means, because you'll be living on the limitless resources of God.